Rosa Luxemburg

Rosa Luxemburg

Harry Harmer

HAUS PUBLISHING · LONDON

First published in Great Britain in 2008 by
Haus Publishing Limited
26 Cadogan Court
Draycott Avenue
London SW3 3BX

www.hauspublishing.co.uk

A CIP catalogue record for this book is available from the British Library

ISBN 978-1-905791-29-3

Typeset in Garamond 3 by MacGuru Ltd
info@macguru.org.uk

Printed at NPT Offset Press Pvt Ltd, India. Email: sales@nptoffset.com
Front cover: Topham Picturepoint

Contents

For my Mother, Ruby Harmer

At your age I didn't play with dolls, I made the revolution 1871–90

Rosa Luxemburg was born Rozalia Luksenburg on 5 March 1871, the year of the Paris Commune, the first major working class revolt. Poland, the country of her birth, was divided in the 18th century by three empires – the Russian, Austrian and German. Rozalia was born a subject of Tsar Alexander II. The adult Luxemburg said little about her childhood, but writing from a prison cell in her thirties she described a younger self gazing from the window across a courtyard towards the rising sun. *I firmly believed that 'life', 'real' life, was somewhere far away, beyond the roofs. Since then I have been travelling after it. But it is still hidden away behind roofs somewhere … In the end it was all a cruel game with me, and life, real life, stayed there in the yard.*[1]

The life Rozalia actually lived was secluded but comfortably middle class. Her parents were Jews striving for assimilation, never completely accepted by their predominantly Catholic neighbours nor entirely trusted by the Orthodox Jewish community. But assimilating into what – Poland, Russia, or the German culture the family so admired? The adult Luxemburg tried to reconcile the conundrum through 'internationalism', with a Marxism that rejected national sentiment. The Luksenburg fortunes ebbed and flowed but were never less than adequate, providing servants, the trappings of a liberal culture and a substantial education for the children. One went on to teach languages, one became a doctor, one

Elias Luksenburg, Rosa's father.

an economist, while the fourth would direct the family business. Rozalia chose a less conventional career.

The Luksenburgs lived in Zamosc, a market town with a major Jewish settlement. A constant Russian military presence maintained the martial law imposed following the abortive Polish national uprising of 1863. Their two-storey house sat impressively in the main square opposite the town hall. Rozalia was the

Rosa's mother Lina.

youngest of five children, and the favourite, a status that persisted into adulthood. Her sister, Anna, had been born in 1858, followed two years later by Mikolaj, and two further brothers, Maksymilian in 1866 and Jozef in 1868.

Rozalia's paternal grandfather had built up a substantial timber enterprise, trading east into Russia and west into Germany. He sent his sons to commercial schools in Berlin, intending them to absorb Germany's modern methods and less restrictive culture. Rozalia's father, Elias, inherited the firm. Much of his business was conducted in Yiddish, but at home the family spoke Polish and German. In later life Rozalia gave the impression that she was closest to her father, identifying with his earnest intelligence and practical energy. She admired her brothers, but admitted she had shown little respect or affection to her sister, the least intellectually able of the family. *I was always irritated, impatient, insufferable.*[2]

She showed a similar attitude towards her mother. Lina Luksenburg (née Löwenstein) was the daughter and sister of rabbis. She continued to observe Jewish festivals after her marriage, more as an excuse for family celebrations than for their religious significance. As an adult, Rozalia dismissed what she saw as her mother's all too typical sacrifice of her own interests for those of her husband and children. She was well educated, which may even have made the sacrifice appear all the worse. She read German as well as Polish literature, with a particular affection for Schiller's idealistic verse, which damned him in Rozalia's eyes. She later told a friend, *I took an instinctive dislike to him because my mother was so crazy about him. By that very fact he was labelled as old-fashioned and sentimental as far as I was concerned.*[3] But she would also speak of her mother indulging her in a glass of Haute-Sauternes to ease a sombre mood.

Whichever of her parents had the greater influence, the adult Luxemburg neglected them equally. Her mother died in 1897, asking repeatedly on her deathbed for Rozalia to return home. A year later Luxemburg wrote that she was thinking constantly of her mother. *The thought that gnaws me is, What was that life about? What was it for? Was it worth living? I know no other thought as dreadful as that. It tears me apart.*[4] She did not see her father for a decade after leaving Poland, and then only for a brief holiday in 1899. In 1900, his death a few months away, his letters ignored, he wrote bitterly, 'Your total indifference reminds me of something I once read. An eagle soars so high he loses all sight of the earth below. You are so busy with social causes that family affairs are not worth even a thought of yours … I won't burden you anymore with my letters.'[5]

~

In 1873 the Luksenburgs moved to Warsaw, for reasons that are not altogether clear. Warsaw housed the largest Jewish population of any European city, 90,000 when the family arrived, over 200,000 by 1890. The move may have been connected with business, the need for greater educational opportunities for the children, or even a desire on Elias Luksenburg's part to escape the confines of small-town Jewry. The family rented a flat at 16 Zlota Street, smaller than the house in Zamosc, but more expensive.

Educated at home by her mother, Rozalia could read and write by the age of five, composing letters to her brothers and sister, demanding they took her seriously enough to reply. She tried to pass on her skills to the family servants, treating them as her pupils. In her fifth year doctors wrongly diagnosed a dislocation of the hip as tuberculosis of the bone, confining her to bed for a year, her leg in a cast. When she was allowed up, one leg was shorter than the other. She was to limp for the rest of her life, blaming her parents for not realising the cause from the beginning. 'She dreaded the street, the strangers, the compassion,' one writer noted. 'All her energy was concentrated on minimizing the limp; it was a triumph to pass in the street unnoticed.'[6]

At the age of 10 Rozalia began full-time education at the Russian Second High School for Girls. The school had a good reputation, catering for the daughters of Russian administrators and middle-class Poles, with a restricted quota of Jews. Most of the instructors were Russian and teaching was in the Russian language. Hampered physically by her limp and the smallest in her class, Rozalia devoted herself to study, reading and writing intensely. She

Rozalia Luksenburg when at school in Warsaw.

was encouraged by her parents but, despite the close cheerfulness of home life and her own bright nature, she felt a growing lack of sympathy with what she saw as their narrow interests.

A photograph of Rozalia aged 16 shows a watchful, wary but self-possessed young woman. The High School banned the use of Polish, even in private conversations between pupils, generating an underground sense of resentment among the Poles and assimilated Jews. On 14 June 1887 Rozalia graduated with As in 14 subjects and Bs in five but was denied the traditional gold medal because of her rebellious attitude. She wrote to a friend at the time, *My ideal is a social system that allows one to love everybody with a clear conscience. Striving after it, defending it, I may perhaps even learn to hate.*[7] The obvious ambiguity suggests a developed political awareness.

In September 1882 the first Polish Marxist party, Proletariat, had been established. Polish capitalism was booming, fuelled by industrial expansion in the Russian Empire, but the workers producing the wealth had little share in it and reacted accordingly. Within a year of the party's foundation, Proletariat had organised strikes in Warsaw and Lodz and a general strike in Zyrardow. The authorities moved to crush the party, arresting and imprisoning leading members. In January 1886 four of them were hanged in the Warsaw Citadel. The remnants of Proletariat went underground, attempting to re-establish the party, an activity Rozalia joined after her high school graduation in 1887. She never explained in her writings why and how she took this step. She now had her first systematic contact with the works of Marx and Engels, with 'scientific socialism', and with the romantic allure of revolutionary conspiracy, for which she developed an enthusiasm. What conjecture there is about her activity is unreliable, but in later years she told a friend's 10-year-old daughter, with obvious exaggeration, *At your age I didn't play with dolls, I made the revolution.*[8]

~

Karl Marx produced a complex and sophisticated body of work, but three basic propositions stood out: the struggle between classes, the eventual collapse of capitalism, and a transition to socialism (or communism, the terms were interchangeable) led by the proletariat, the working class. His closest comrade, Frederick Engels, had no doubt that Marx had found the key to historical development. In his funeral ovation in 1883 Engels said, 'Just as Darwin had discovered the law of development of organic nature so did Marx discover the law of human history.'[9]

The Communist Manifesto, written by Marx and Engels in 1848, declared, 'The history of all hitherto existing society is the history of class struggles'. Marx's economic analysis, which grew more complex over time, sought to explain how capitalism worked and the theoretical limits to its survival, while his description of communism told how the world should and would be. From feudalism had emerged a bourgeois class that developed industrial capitalism, superseding feudalism and winning political power through revolution. Capitalism fashioned the proletariat that would, in its turn, replace the bourgeoisie and institute communism. 'Of all the classes that stand face to face with the bourgeoisie today, the proletariat alone is a really revolutionary class.' Communists 'openly declare that their ends can be obtained only by the forcible overthrow of all existing social conditions. Let the ruling classes tremble at a communist revolution. The proletarians have nothing to lose but their chains. They have a world to win. Workingmen of all countries, unite!'[10]

That was clear enough, but the sophisticated layers of Marx's thinking perplexed his followers. There was, for example, the question of nationalism, which had some importance in the context of occupied Poland. Marx and Engels said in *The Communist Manifesto*, 'The workingmen have no country ... National differences between people are daily more and more vanishing.'[11] But at the same time the working class would have to engage with the bourgeoisie in their own country. What did that mean for a Poland divided in three? Proletariat had opposed a struggle for national independence, arguing that Poland was not one nation but an arena for contending classes. Marx would have agreed, theoretically, but he considered, tactically, that for the Poles to regain their sovereignty would strike a blow against the occupying empires of Russia ('the Mongols' as he called them), Prussia and Austria. The members of Proletariat, as 'Russian' Poles, disagreed: the only legitimate struggle was that of a united working class throughout the Russian Empire. Luxemburg retained Proletariat's 'internationalism' throughout her life.

A second problem Marx's work posed was the collapse of capitalism. Inevitable, perhaps, but when? As one academic economist has neatly observed, 'Marx was an astronomer of history, not an astrologer.'[12] In 1859 he gave a major clue, though it was not published until after his death. 'No social order ever disappears before all the productive forces for which there is room in it have been developed; and new higher relations of production never appear before the material conditions of their existence have matured in the womb of the old society itself.'[13] Capitalism would not break down until it had fully played itself out and socialism would not emerge until the time was right. One question nagged at Luxemburg and other socialists into the 20th century – was it necessary to wait patiently for the historical process to unfold or could action speed the collapse? If you know how the story ends, why not cut to the conclusion? As Luxemburg herself was to write, *We are a party of class struggle, not 'historical laws'.*[14]

Rozalia's direct political engagement was short-lived but set the scene for the remainder of her life. In February 1889 she travelled to Switzerland and would not return to Poland until 1905. One story has been repeated about Rozalia's decision to leave – that the police were pursuing her as a revolutionary and she fled, hiding under straw in a peasant's wagon. In another version she persuaded a Roman Catholic priest to smuggle her out after convincing him she was escaping her family to convert to Christianity. Both are implausible. Rozalia's parents were determined to secure the best education for their children, particularly the daughter expected to outshine her siblings. Poland did not allow women a university education; Swiss universities accepted students regardless of sex or nationality. On 5 March 1888 the authorities had issued Rozalia with a passport to enable her to leave Poland.

Rozalia formally registered as a resident in Zurich on 18 February 1889 under the name 'Rosa Luxemburg' but did not begin her studies until October. Luxemburg spent her first months in the new city with the Lübeck family. Karl Lübeck was a German socialist, forced into exile by the Anti-Socialist Laws. Half blind, he struggled to support his family by journalism. His wife, Olympia, who had been born in Poland, was mother to eight children. From Olympia Luxemburg gained friendship; from Karl, whom she helped prepare articles, she gained a deeper knowledge of West European, and particularly German, socialism. Zurich had been the home of Karl Kautsky, Wilhelm Liebknecht, August Bebel and Eduard Bernstein – all exiles like Lübeck and major figures in German socialism who would play a part in Luxemburg's life.

Luxemburg would later say that she passed some of her happiest days in Zurich. With its genuinely cosmopolitan atmosphere, the university had become the 'alma mater of young revolutionaries'.[15] Luxemburg met the founders of the first Russian Marxist party, Liberation of Labour, Georgii Plekhanov, Vera Zasulich (who had tried unsuccessfully to assassinate a general), and Pavel Axelrod. Intimidated by Plekhanov's political sophistication at their first meeting, Luxemburg wrote to a friend, *What could he possibly gain from a conversation with me? He knows everything better than I do, and I cannot create 'ideas' – original, genuine ideas.*[16]

Luxemburg registered at the university in natural science, taking a course in the principles of zoology over the winter of 1889–90. In 1891 she moved to more politically-oriented studies, taking courses in political economy, modern and classical philosophy and law, working intensely. Her main professor later wrote of the satisfaction he felt at having given a solid academic foundation 'to the ablest of my pupils during my time at Zurich, Rosa

Luxemburg, even though she came to me from Poland already as a thorough Marxist'.[17] Luxemburg maintained her connections with Polish socialism through a fellow student, Adolf Warski, but Leo Jogiches, whom she met at the end of 1890, was to have the greatest impact on her life, politically and personally.

The 23-year-old's reputation as a dedicated revolutionary caught Luxemburg's attention at once. Born in 1867 in Wilno, Lithuania, Jogiches rebelled against his wealthy Jewish business family by leaving school at 16 without graduating, briefly working for a locksmith. Much of his early life remains a mystery, but there are hints of involvement with the Russian terrorist group People's Will. Living on his family's money, Jogiches devoted his time to politics, organising a strike at a printing works in 1888, earning a short prison term. He was conscripted into the army on his release but deserted in 1890, fleeing to Switzerland. When Luxemburg became aware of his urge to dominate she told him, *The whole world is not full of idiots who, as you think, understand only when bashed over the head with a club.*[18]

Luise Kautsky, one of Luxemburg's closest women friends, had no doubt about the initial attraction. Jogiches, she wrote, 'was a master in the art of plotting, the romanticism of which cast an irresistible spell upon Rosa's impressionable mind'. Luxemburg, she believed, craved this 'if life was not to seem flat and "petty bourgeois" to her'.[19] But what was Luxemburg's attraction to Jogiches? One of his friends described her at the time they met. 'She was of low build, with a disproportionately large head; a typical Jewish face with a thick nose … a heavy, occasionally uneven, walk, with a limp; her first appearance did not make an agreeable impression but you had only to spend a bit of time with her to see how much life and energy was in the woman, how clever and sharp she was, and at what a high level of intellectual stimulation and development she lived.'[20]

Luxemburg's disability made her doubt her attractiveness to

men. Years later that sensitivity remained. *Good God, if I sense in the slightest that somebody doesn't like me, my very thoughts flee from his presence like those of a scared bird; for me even to look him in the face again seems too much.*[21] Jogiches respected her intellect (of which Luxemburg was legitimately, even arrogantly, proud) and she his reputation, which he burnished like a trophy. But it was apparent early on that a mismatch in desires and expectations generated a maze of frustrations and misunderstandings. On the surface, their personalities differed radically. Luxemburg was bright, cheerful and expansive, Jogiches dour, rigid and closed; she was by far the more sensual. But they were equal in their self-centredness, with temperaments that made co-operation with others difficult.

I neither exist nor live as myself 1891–8

Jogiches had another attraction – regular payments from his family. Luxemburg's parents supported her studies, but Jogiches ensured there were no financial worries. Her letters to him over many years – over a thousand in all – are scattered with requests, frequently demands, for money to buy clothes or pleas for him to pay her rent. When Luxemburg told Jogiches, *People's primary concern is to support themselves and their children or their parents, and only then should they think of becoming great scholars*, she expressed an idea, not something she had experienced herself.[22] Jogiches's remittances from Lithuania enabled her to study and write, and him to conspire and indulge his taste for well-tailored suits, without the need to seriously consider earning a living.

Luxemburg and Jogiches became lovers in the summer of 1891. She left the Lübecks' house in the autumn, taking a second-floor flat at 77 Universitätsstrasse on a hill overlooking the university. Jogiches rented a room in the house next door. In July Luxemburg had written to a friend in Poland that she was now *really a mature person, which makes me very proud of myself.* But Jogiches insisted the fact they were a couple should be kept secret, not only from her family but from even their closest political acquaintances, though there was inevitably gossip in the close-knit socialist circles. Seven years on, Luxemburg was to complain *To go on pretending about our relationship is not just overdoing it; it is simply hypocritical.*[23] Nevertheless, they continued to live separately, being together only when they took holidays.

A year after his arrival in Switzerland, bored and frustrated, Jogiches visited the couple's mutual acquaintance Plekhanov in Geneva seeking membership of Liberation of Labour, the Marxist party in which the Russian had been a leading light since 1883. Jogiches's personal arrogance was buoyed up by his wealth and he proposed that the party should publish a socialist journal, which he would finance and direct. This was effectively a suggestion for a major share in the control of Liberation of Labour. Plekhanov, understanding completely what Jogiches was after, rejected his offer, dismissing him as a 'careerist'. Jogiches would hardly have impressed as an editor, Luxemburg herself once saying, *His brilliance and intelligence notwithstanding, Leo is simply unable to write. The mere thought of putting his ideas on paper paralyzes him.*[24] Rebuffed, Jogiches fell deeper into isolation, while Luxemburg became by default an enemy of Plekhanov's. The solution, it became clear, was for Luxemburg and Jogiches to form a party of their own.

In 1892 Luxemburg transferred to the university law department, which included political science, where she was to remain for the next five years. Jogiches, berated by Luxemburg for his laziness, reluctantly registered for botany and zoology, but he would never be more than a nominal student. Devoted as she remained to her studies, and talented as she clearly was, Luxemburg's real interest was politics. In 1892 West European émigré groups established a Polish Socialist Party (PPS), hoping to unite the competing strands, those who sought national independence and those who put the international working class struggle for socialism first. The argument was purely theoretical and involved only intellectuals. There seemed little possibility in the foreseeable future of a Polish national rising, or a revolt by the Russian Empire's tiny working class. The dispute nevertheless persisted and at the end of the year the Paris-based Association of Polish Socialists Abroad, which had a majority in the PPS, pressed again for a policy based on nationalism.

The battle was fought out in front of delegates to the congress of the Socialist International in 1893. An International Workingmen's Association (the First International) had been established in London in 1864 but collapsed, torn by disputes between the libertarian Anarchists, led by Mikhail Bakunin, and the authoritarian Marxists, led by Marx. While the Marxists envisaged a strong state after the revolution, as a preliminary to communism (when the state would have 'withered away'), the Anarchists argued that state domination was no improvement on capitalism. They had doubts too about the role Marxist intellectuals were creating for themselves. Bakunin warned in 1872 that 'the rule of the new society by socialist savants is the worst of all despotic governments'.[25]

'Our aim,' the Socialist International's founding charter said, 'is the emancipation of the workers, the abolition of wage-labour and the creation of a society in which all women and men irrespective of sex or nationality will enjoy the wealth produced by all the workers.'[26] The Socialist International's recognition of a party was an important symbol of political credibility on the left. Nevertheless, rules for affiliation to the body were loose: merely publishing a regular newspaper was taken as evidence that a party was functioning.

Socialist (Second) International

The successor to the International Working Men's Association (the First International) formed by Marx in 1864 and dissolved in 1876, the Socialist International was established in 1889 as a forum for exchange of information between member parties. Until 1914 the German Social Democratic Party (Sozialdemokratische Partei Deutschlands – SPD) was the strongest and most influential member. The Socialist International effectively collapsed at the outbreak of the First World War, when socialist parties supported their national governments rather than opposing the conflict. In 1919 Lenin established the Communist (Third) International. In 1923 the Socialist International was re-established as the Labour and Socialist International and reverted to its original name after the Second World War.

Georgi Plekhanov (1856–1918).

On 18 July 1893, a month before the congress, Luxemburg and Jogiches, joined by Adolf Warski and Julian Marchlewski (the latter only recently at liberty after a year in a Warsaw prison for his activities in the Union of Polish Workers), published the first edition of *The Workers' Cause*. The strategy was Jogiches's but its public face was Luxemburg's and she – using the name Kruszynska – put the case for the group's recognition to the congress, conveniently held that year in Zurich. Making her first appearance before an audience, Luxemburg showed a remarkable confidence, accusing the delegates – the elite of European socialism – of failing to comprehend the Polish situation. Striving for national independence was, Luxemburg told the congress, a diversion from the real needs of the working class and from its historic destiny. *People understand that the economic struggles for the daily interests of the working class, and the struggle for a democratic form of government, are a school through which the proletariat must necessarily pass before becoming capable of overthrowing the present social order.*[27]

The Association's speakers responded contemptuously, one saying Luxemburg had no feeling for Poland's thirst for liberty

because she was a Jew. They scoffed at the idea that *The Workers'
Cause*, of which only one thin issue had so far appeared, was worthy
of the Socialist International's notice. Plekhanov, not surprisingly,
backed the Association, accusing Jogiches privately of using his
mistress to try to seize control of the Polish movement. There were
whispers behind the scenes that some individuals around the paper
were police agents.

The leading Belgian socialist Emile Vandervelde wrote a vivid
description of Luxemburg's performance. 'I can see her now: how
she sprang to her feet out of the sea of delegates and jumped onto
a chair to make herself better heard. Small, delicate and dainty in
a summer dress which cleverly concealed her physical defects, she
advocated her cause with such magnetism in her eyes and with such
fiery words that she enthralled and won over the great majority of
the congress, who raised their hands in favour of the acceptance
of their mandate.'[28] In fact, the delegates, impressed though they
must have been by Luxemburg's brilliance as a speaker, rejected
what she said and welcomed the Association as the authentic
Polish Socialist Party.

Disappointed by the Socialist International's response,
Luxemburg, Jogiches, Marchlewski and Warski began preparing
for the next congress in 1896, transforming what had been a
newspaper into a thoroughgoing party, the Social Democracy of
the Kingdom of Poland (SDKP), a name chosen by Luxemburg.
The SDKP held its founding meeting in Zurich in March 1894,
agreeing a set of minimum and maximum demands drafted
by Luxemburg. The final objective was social revolution, the
overthrow of capitalism by the working class, but in the shorter
term the party sought a liberal constitution for Russia and
autonomy (rather than independence) for Poland. The SDKP was
in reality no more than a group of friends – a small business masquerading as a large corporation – gathered round two dominant,
and domineering, personalities: Jogiches, supplying the finance

and direction, and Luxemburg, putting the agitational steam into *The Workers' Cause*.

Luxemburg edited and contributed the majority of articles to the party's paper, under a variety of names. A letters column tried to persuade the few readers they were part of a wide and enthusiastic audience, but Luxemburg wrote most of them herself. *The Workers' Cause* claimed a large circulation throughout Poland, but there was, for example, only one supporter in the whole of Warsaw. The paper ceased publication with issue 24 in June 1896 and the SDKP itself did not hold another congress until 1900. Directed from Switzerland, by students with only minimal support in Poland – where nationalism was genuinely popular – the SDKP was in reality a device for gaining entry to the Socialist International. This did not mean that Luxemburg and Jogiches were not serious about the ideas they put forward; they were and would develop them over the years.

～

In early 1894 Luxemburg left Zurich to conduct research in a library in Paris. She also oversaw the production of the party paper, which was printed in France. Luxemburg's letters to Jogiches (none of his have survived) reveal wavering feelings about the state of their life together, the constant arguing, Jogiches's domineering nature, his resentment of her friends, his criticisms of her appearance, his unwillingness or inability to show affection; but, at the same time, they show her persistent regard for him. Often their letters are the relationship, held together by the party in which they were investing their lives and Luxemburg's attempts to persuade Jogiches that they were, in her words, 'husband' and 'wife'.

On 25 March Luxemburg unleashed her anger with Jogiches. *Your letters contain nothing, but nothing except for The Workers' Cause, criticism of what I have done, and instructions about what I should do ...*

I want you to write me about your personal life. But not a single word! Our only ties are the Cause and the memory of old feelings. That is very painful. She told Jogiches she had been thinking about her life. *I looked back and realised I don't have a home anywhere. I neither exist nor live as myself ... I don't want to stay here or go back to Zurich ... It's a burden – every letter, from you or anyone else, always the same – this issue, that pamphlet, this article or that. Even that I wouldn't mind if besides, despite it, there was a human being behind it, a soul, an individual. But for you there's nothing, nothing but 'The Cause'.* She concluded with a detailed account of where money Jogiches had sent was going. *Unfortunately I'm spending a lot of money, don't know how.*[29] In a week her mood had changed and she was tempted to leap on a train at the Gare de L'Est and rush to him.

A year later, once more in Paris, Luxemburg complained Jogiches showed the feelings of a stone. Reading between the lines of Luxemburg's letters, their sexual relationship seemed intermittent and, to her, far from satisfactory. *Once it was done – proved in word and deed – that you love me, you acted like you loved me. But inside you, you feel nothing, no natural impulse to love ... Mention the PPS, and your eyes light up. Write about myself, that I'm tired, that I miss you, and it's quite different.* But one plea remained constant. *Darlingest, please send me some money for my expenses! At once.*[30]

Luxemburg's next letter set out her dreams of a future life together: sleeping and rising early, surrounded with elegant possessions and, above all, no arguments. *These fights turn our whole life upside down. We'll work regularly and peacefully. I'll agree to all your demands concerning my looks and our home (but not my relations with people, however!) ... I have made up my mind to start living like a human being, and should you frustrate my plans, I'll hang myself.* Why was it, she asked, that her life in Paris had some order? *Because I'm not constantly frantic, disheartened, driven crazy by you. Be good, and I'll do my best to make us a nice home. Only be good and love me, and then everything will be fine.*[31]

Luxemburg worked busily in Paris researching her doctoral thesis, writing articles for *The Workers' Cause* and acquainting herself with the leading personalities in French socialism. In February 1895 she produced a pamphlet on the Polish national question, continuing the argument with the Polish Socialist Party. In March 1896 she submitted an article on the same issue to *Die Neue Zeit*, the theoretical journal of the German social democratic party, the SPD. She asked the editor, Karl Kautsky, who had established the journal in 1893, to correct any errors he found. *Since the German language is a foreign tongue to me, it is quite possible that an incorrect expression may have crept in here or there.*[32] While he disagreed with her analysis, Kautsky admired the clarity and force with which she expressed her heretical views and published the article, which the Italian socialist journal, *Critica Sociale*, then reprinted. Luxemburg's purpose had been served: preparing opinion for the SDKP's next attempt to gain entry to the Socialist International.

Luxemburg led the SDKP group at the Socialist International congress, which opened in London in July 1896. Backed by what was, on the surface, a party organisation with a newspaper (but which, unknown to the delegates, had ceased publication a month before), her credentials were accepted and the SDKP became an official member of the Socialist International, along with the Polish Socialist Party. The dispute about nationalism rolled on, Luxemburg telling the congress that Polish independence was *a utopian mirage, a delusion of the workers to distract them from their class struggle.* An opponent replied that the Socialist International was making a serious mistake if it was prepared to tolerate 'scribblers and crooks like Rosa Luxemburg ... a journalistic brigand'.[33]

Luxemburg was now a recognised figure on the international socialist stage, addressing the 1893 and 1896 congresses, her articles appearing more frequently in the press, particularly that of the SPD. Kautsky encouraged further contributions on Polish politics. Influence in Germany, the heart of European Marxism, was crucial and the contacts Luxemburg had made in Switzerland began to pay off. In 1896 Marchlewski, a co-founder of the SDKP, became an editor of the Dresden-based daily *Sächsiche Arbeiterzeitung*. His co-editor was Alexander Parvus-Helphand, a Russian Marxist with whom Luxemburg had also become friendly in Zurich. Commissions began to flow from Dresden and within 18 months Luxemburg had written over 50 articles for the German socialist press. Proud of her achievements, Luxemburg sent cuttings to her family. Her sister Anna wrote, with a touch of sarcasm, 'Did you make a mistake, or is that how you now spell your name? I saw the change in N Zeit and was surprised.'[34]

Luxemburg and Jogiches were working to a well thought-out political strategy: first, acceptance by the Socialist International; second, influence in the most prominent party in the Socialist International, the SPD. Luxemburg was building a reputation, leaving Jogiches – who had seen himself at the outset as her mentor in revolution – a frustrated spectator, as she recognised. In July 1896 she wrote to him, somewhat cruelly, *My success and the public recognition I'm getting are likely to poison our relationship because of your pride and suspicion. The further I go the worse it will get.*[35]

In 1899 Feliks Dzierzynski persuaded the Union of Workers in Lithuania to adopt the SDKP's position on nationalism. Dzierzynski was subsequently to become a Bolshevik and, after the 1917 revolution, head of the Soviet secret police, the Cheka. In 1900 the Lithuanian party and the SDKP formally merged to form the Social Democratic Party of the Kingdom of Poland and Lithuania (SDKPiL). Dzierzynski's arrest in 1901 enabled Jogiches and Luxemburg to take complete control of the party.

~

In April 1897 Luxemburg's mother was diagnosed with stomach cancer, barely managing the pain with morphine. Luxemburg's sister, Anna, wrote regularly, keeping her up-to-date with developments, making it obvious she thought Luxemburg was neglecting her mother. Luxemburg was preoccupied by more pressing matters. On 1 May 1897 she was awarded a doctorate in law and political science for her thesis, 'The Industrial Development of Poland', and a publisher had accepted it as a book. At the same time German socialists acclaimed an article she had written for *Die Neue Zeit*, 'Step by Step: The History of the Bourgeois Classes in Poland' for its sophisticated analysis. Luxemburg's parents – who continued to send her 10 roubles a month – were delighted at the news of their daughter's academic success and her mother asked persistently when she would visit. Anna wrote, 'I had no choice. In order to calm her down I promised her you'd come.'[36] Luxemburg remained in Zurich.

In July Luxemburg wrote to Jogiches, who was living in the house next door. *We live only ten steps apart and meet three times a day – and anyway, I'm only your wife – why then the romanticism, writing in the middle of the night to my own husband?* She said it was because she felt uneasy, unable to talk to him directly about what mattered to her. It pained her that he saw their relationship as superficial. *It is probably my fault, more mine than yours, that our relationship is not warm, smooth. What can I do? I don't know, I don't know how to act … Now everything I do is wrong. You find fault with me no matter what. You don't seem to have much need to be with me …*[37]

But they clung together, spending all of September on holiday in a village by Lake Lucerne. On 30 September Luxemburg's mother died, conscious and calling for her daughter. Luxemburg could not be contacted, at Jogiches's insistence, and did not know of her mother's death until their return to Zurich. Her remorse took a singularly selfish turn. Luxemburg's father and sister, still unaware of Jogiches's existence and fearing she would be alone in her anguish, said they would come to Zurich. Luxemburg discouraged them, saying she might be leaving Switzerland. But she wrote again the same day saying she had nothing to live for now her mother was dead, distressing her father, who replied that he could not bear to lose both his wife and daughter. Anna wrote angrily to her sister. 'How can you, how dare you to even entertain such thoughts! You must never forget mother's words – that you alone will make our family's name famous.'[38]

Luxemburg had not been entirely untruthful about leaving Switzerland, which she had been considering for some time. Moving to Germany, which Marxists considered the most likely country to undergo a socialist revolution, had been implicit in the couple's strategy since at least 1896. In July of that year Luxemburg shared her concerns with Jogiches over the possible impact on their relationship. *If, after mature consideration, I should come to the conclusion that I either have to withdraw from the movement and live in peace with you in some godforsaken hole, or else move the world but live in torment with you, I would choose the latter.*[39] She had every intention of seizing her opportunities, but re-assured him of her feelings when arrangements to go to Germany were well advanced. *You have no idea with what joy and desire I wait for every letter from you because each one brings me so much strength and happiness and encourages me to live.*[40] In 1900 Luxemburg was to describe their relationship entirely differently. *Even in Zurich we were spiritual strangers and the frightful loneliness of these last two years is engraved on my mind.*[41]

With a ruthless practicality which Jogiches would have admired and probably encouraged, the 27-year-old Luxemburg went through a marriage ceremony with the 25-year-old Gustav Lübeck in Basel on 19 April 1898. Lübeck was a son of the socialist couple, Karl and Olympia Lübeck, who had looked after Luxemburg when she first arrived in Zurich. The union was one of convenience, easing Luxemburg's move to Germany by giving her citizenship. The couple parted at the door of the register office, never to meet again, and the marriage was dissolved in 1903. Luxemburg kept her new status from her family in Warsaw. On 16 May Luxemburg arrived in Berlin by train. Jogiches stayed in Zurich, correcting the proofs of her book, *The Industrial Development of Poland*, promising to join her as soon as he could.

I shall occupy a position at the top of the party 1898–1902

The Germany in which Luxemburg arrived had the strongest and most influential socialist and trade union movement in Europe. The German Social Democratic Party (Sozialdemokratische Partei Deutschlands – SPD) had been established in 1875. In 1878 the Imperial Chancellor, Otto von Bismarck, banned the party, alarmed that it had won seats in elections to the Reichstag. He tried to dampen the attraction of socialism with kindness, bribing the growing industrial working class with the beginnings of a welfare state. Over 1,500 members were arrested or driven into exile before the SPD was allowed to resume open activity in 1890.

In October 1891 the SPD adopted the Erfurt Programme, drafted by August Bebel Eduard Bernstein and Karl Kautsky, the 'Pope of Marxism'. Bebel and Kautsky had been close to Marx and Engels, the fathers of scientific socialism. The programme set out 'maximum' and 'minimum' demands – reform in the short term and revolution in the long term. The ultimate objective was the social ownership of the means of production following the collapse of capitalism, which was both inevitable and – the programme's language implied – imminent. Kautsky was at pains to explain – for legal reasons as well as personal preference – that 'revolution' did not mean armed revolt. 'In this sense of the word the socialist party has never been revolutionary in principle ... [But] on the day it obtains political power it can use it in no other way but to destroy the mode of production upon which the social order of today rests.'[42] Until the time was ripe, the party would pursue its minimum objectives – genuine parliamentary democracy, a universal adult franchise, a welfare state financed by graduated income tax, an eight-hour working day, prohibition of child labour and free education.

While gaining these reforms, the party's intelligentsia would educate the working class in the necessity of the ultimate socialist goal. But a contradiction ran through the SPD's activity. Though Bebel, who co-wrote the programme, might say, 'I am and always will be a mortal enemy of existing society',[43] achieving the party's minimum demands presupposed a thriving capitalist system, not an economy always on the edge of crisis. If the party could not win these reforms, which involved an accommodation with the system Bebel described as the 'enemy', what attraction would it have to voters and members? And if it could, the working class might ask what was wrong with capitalism.

There was also the question of how far SPD members themselves understood the nuances of Marxism. Kautsky wrote a commentary on Erfurt entitled *The Class Struggle*, simplifying scientific socialism for a popular audience.

Karl Kautsky (1854–1938)

Born in Prague, Kautsky's status as the leading Marxist theoretician of the SPD and Socialist International – he founded and edited the journal *Die Neue Zeit* – earned him the soubriquet 'The Pope of Marxism'. A friend of Engels, Kautsky joined the Austrian Social Democrats in 1875 and was active in the pre-1890 illegal German socialist movement, his *The Economic Doctrines of Karl Marx* (1887) popularising Marxism. Kautsky led the 'Marxist Centre', straddling the division between 'revisionism' and Luxemburg's radicalism, emphasising a democratic transition to socialism. He joined the anti-war Independent Social Democrats in 1917, opposed the 1917 Bolshevik coup in Russia, and rejoined the SPD in 1922. He left Germany in 1933, fled Austria when it came under Nazi control in 1938 and died in Amsterdam.

Most party members probably did not read much further. One study suggests the majority 'either failed to understand Marxism or take it seriously. At best, they believed in a series of vulgar Marxist dogmas … without understanding the connections between them.'[44] As if that were not enough, Marx had dismissed Kautsky, on whom the SPD depended for theoretical coherence, as 'a small-minded mediocrity, too clever by half, industrious in a certain way, busying himself with statistics from which he does not derive anything intelligent, belonging by nature to the tribe of Philistines'.[45]

Dominated by the Prussian military caste, Germany was far from being a functioning democracy. Bismarck had successfully detached nationalism from its 19th-century partner liberalism, leaving an inheritance of authoritarianism, militarism, anti-socialism and anti-Catholicism. The voting system was hedged around with qualifications and restricted to men. The Imperial Chancellor and ministers were responsible to the Kaiser, not to the Reichstag deputies. Although legal since 1890, the SPD remained an outlaw in establishment eyes. Kaiser Wilhelm II warned that in the unlikely event of securing a Reichstag majority, the party would 'at once proceed to plunder the citizens'.[46] No party meeting could proceed without a police officer keeping watch and taking notes of speeches. The government banned its employees from joining the party and forbade the sale of SPD newspapers at railway station newsstands. So reactionary and contemptuous of democracy were most deputies that they cheered a conservative who told them, 'The King of Prussia and the German Emperor must always be in a position to say to any lieutenant, "Take ten men and shoot the Reichstag".'[47]

～

Adolf Warski, Luxemburg's comrade from the SDKPiL, and his

wife greeted Luxemburg on her arrival in Berlin, complimenting her on the dress and hat she had worn for the journey. She told Jogiches she felt guilty about how much the dress had cost him. Jogiches made her an allowance of 100 marks a month and Luxemburg spent the first day seeking lodgings, taking a room first at 55 Kantstrasse and then settling at 2 Cuxhavenstrasse, a prosperous street near the Tiergarten. *The washbasin in the corner is hardly noticeable, elegant furniture, a grand piano, and I had the floor polished in the best Swiss style. Facing the garden is a vine-overgrown balcony with a small table and chairs. Once the books and Beethoven arrive, I can safely receive whomever I please (there's also a hanging lamp and a desk).*[48]

The fissures in their relationship remained and in one letter Luxemburg resumed an argument she had had with Jogiches the evening before she left Switzerland. *Despite everything you told me before I left, I keep harping on my worn-out tune, making claims on personal happiness. Yes, I do have a cursed longing for happiness and am ready to haggle for my daily portion with the stubbornness of a mule. But I'm losing it … I feel like a forty-year-old woman going through the symptoms of menopause … Do you have any idea how much I love you?* Then she slipped into conspiratorial mode, warning Jogiches that spies were constantly around. In the margin she wrote that she was asking her father for a loan.[49]

Luxemburg found Berlin unimpressive after Zurich, writing to a Polish friend, *Berlin is the most repulsive place: cold, ugly, massive – a real barracks, and the charming Prussians with their arrogance as if each one of them had been made to swallow the very stick with which he had got his daily beating.*[50] It was not just the oppressive atmosphere: she was confronted in Berlin by a double prejudice among Prussians, who saw both Poles and Jews as irredeemably inferior. Luxemburg had her first introduction to the former at the SPD headquarters, where she presented herself on 25 May. Women were not allowed to join political parties but that did not prevent Luxemburg from offering her services as a writer and speaker to the SPD.

The party secretary, Ignaz Auer, outlined the political situation in German-occupied Poland (which Luxemburg said she understood as well as he did), before asking her to travel at once to the area to address SPD election rallies. Auer confided, 'One could do the Polish workers no bigger favour than to Germanise them. But this should not be mentioned to them.'[51] Luxemburg may have partly agreed, later describing Upper Silesia to the Kautskys as *the boundary between civilisation and barbarism*.[52] Speaking to Poles in obscure mining villages had not been what Luxemburg had envisaged, but she told Jogiches she felt obliged to accept the mission.

To Luxemburg's delight, her progress from meeting to meeting boosted her confidence as a speaker and agitator. She wrote exuberantly to Jogiches at the end of June 1898, *I plunged in, head on, with no idea how it would turn out. Now I'm convinced that in six months I'll be one of the best speakers in the party. My voice, my poise, my language – nothing failed, and, most important, I walked up to the platform without batting an eyelash, as if I had done it for the last twenty years.*[53] The miners, still black with coal dust, flocked about her, asking where she came from, where she had gone to school, where her family lived.

Back in Berlin, Luxemburg asked Jogiches what he thought of the new Russian Social Democratic Labour Party, formed in the spring. *Naturally, just what I do; rascals, and yet they managed it.*[54] But, for herself, she said life was flat and complained of the migraines and stomach cramps that were to afflict her for years to come. But she complained above all that Jogiches was still in Zurich. Jogiches blamed difficulties over obtaining Swiss citizenship but also made it clear he was jealous of the friendships she was making. Bruno Schönlank, the editor of the *Leipziger Volkszeitung*, a popular SPD paper, had asked her to contribute articles

The Reichstag building in Berlin in the late 19th century.

after a conversation on a train. Luxemburg told Jogiches not to be concerned. *I can do with him what I want.*[55]

Luxemburg had arrived as the SPD faced its deepest political crisis since 1890, one threatening to burst open the ambiguity of its programme. Luxemburg would have been aware of this from articles appearing in *Die Neue Zeit* over the previous two years, years in which she had been preparing her move to Germany. Luxemburg and Jogiches would have seen the opportunity emerging to push herself and their politics forwards. In November 1896 Edouard Bernstein had published the first of a series of eight articles on the 'Problems of Socialism' in Kautsky's journal, the last appearing in the summer of 1898. Bernstein had been Engels's secretary until the latter's death in 1895, but what he wrote now threatened to tear Marxism apart.

Bernstein was building on his observations in Britain, where he had lived in exile and where industrial capitalism was at its most advanced. Marx, he said, had failed to see capitalism's flexibility and willingness to adapt. The system's crises gave every sign of diminishing rather than intensifying in force. New institutions and policies – cartels, the credit system, trade unions and co-operatives, social legislation – were easing capitalism's contradictions. Marx had been mistaken in his confidence that the middle class would disappear – rather than being crushed out of existence between the bourgeoisie and the proletariat, it was expanding. The workers, instead of falling into poverty and misery, were prospering. Bernstein urged socialists to renounce the class struggle, abandon any idea of revolution, and collaborate with the liberal middle classes to democratise Germany.

Bernstein did not rule out the possibility that capitalism might some day break down as Marx had prophesied, but that event was so remote it was idle to imagine socialism of the type the SPD advocated and in the way it prophesied emerging in the near future. 'In the modern working-class movement', he wrote, 'what matters is not the sensational battles but the ground gained piecemeal by hard, unremitting struggle.'

Eduard Bernstein (1850–1932)
Born in Berlin, son of a Jewish railway engineer, Bernstein worked in a bank and became a socialist in 1872. In 1878 he moved to Switzerland, where he remained when the socialists were outlawed in Germany. Later moving to London, he became close to Engels and the reformist Fabian Society. Bernstein co-authored the SPD's 1891 Erfurt Programme, but the revisionist theories he set out in articles in 1896 and 1898 and in *Evolutionary Socialism* in 1899 divided the party. He returned to Germany in 1901. A Reichstag deputy from 1902–6 and 1912–18, he voted against war credits in 1915, becoming a leading figure in the Independent Social Democrats in 1917. Economy and finance secretary in the post-revolution government, Bernstein rejoined the SPD and was a Reichstag deputy from 1920 to 1928, strongly opposing the rise of the Nazis.

Evolution rather than revolution, then, a process in which a future SPD government would administer capitalism, reforming where it could. Most damning of all was a phrase that would be thrown in his face. 'I frankly admit that I have extraordinarily little feeling for, or interest in, what is usually called "the final goal of socialism". This goal, whatever it may be, is nothing to me; but the movement is everything.'[56] Socialism was not a destination for Bernstein, but what the party did. For Luxemburg, as for Marx, socialism was the beginning of mankind's real destiny.

Luxemburg's friend Parvus-Helphand launched the first attack on Bernstein's 'revisionism' in his Dresden newspaper, *Sächsiche Arbeiterzeitung*. Others, Luxemburg included, jostled to land the next punch. On 2 July 1898 she asked Jogiches for his advice, making plain the intertwined political and personal ambition involved. *Although I've a good idea about the whole article, I don't feel any better because I also see enormous difficulties. I worked out an excellent outline. There are two difficult problems: (1) to write about crises; (2) to prove beyond doubt that capitalism must break its neck … Help, for heaven's sake, help! Speed is essential because if somebody gets ahead of us the entire work is wasted.*[57] A forceful and early blow against Bernstein would establish her reputation as a party intellectual.

Luxemburg's fear – and the fear of the SPD left in general – was that if Bernstein had read capitalism properly, revolutionary Marxism was redundant. If capitalism could adapt and adapt again, if its contradictions were not chronic, if the system was not fated to 'break its neck', Marxism had no scientific basis. Socialism would be the sentimental utopian dream Marx had despised, rather than an inevitable necessity. Luxemburg finished the first draft of her article at the end of August and it appeared over seven successive issues in the *Leipziger Volkszeitung* from 21–8 September 1898, subsequently collected in book form as *Social Reform or Revolution*.

Luxemburg accepted that the SPD and, to an even greater extent the trade unions, were acting in many ways as Bernstein had suggested they should. Auer, the party secretary, had admitted as much when he wrote to Bernstein, 'One doesn't *say* such things, one simply *does* them.'[58] But what was critical to Luxemburg was that any political and economic gains the party and unions made were a means, not an end. The 'final goal of socialism' was all that distinguished the SPD from other parties, she wrote, *the only factor transforming the entire labour movement from a vain attempt to repair the capitalist order into a class struggle against this order, for the suppression of this order*. She agreed progress might be slower than Marx had implied, but if Bernstein meant that capitalism was not moving inevitably to self-destruction then socialism was no longer objectively necessary. *Either revisionism is correct concerning the course of capitalist development, and therefore the socialist transformation of society becomes a utopia. Or socialism is not a utopia; and therefore the theory of the 'means of adaptation' is false.*[59]

Luxemburg did not deny that in a non-revolutionary period it was necessary to agitate for reforms, but they were part of the same struggle. Different phases of capitalism demanded different tactics. *Legal reform and revolution are not different methods of historical progress that can be picked out at pleasure from the counter of history, just as one chooses hot or cold sausages. They come at different moments in the development of class society.*[60] She dismissed Bernstein as a petty-bourgeois democratic progressive and wondered why he stayed in the SPD. In the snobbish intellectual Marxist world, to be petty bourgeois often seemed a greater offence than being a bourgeois, who might at least have style.

Luxemburg's retort to Bernstein was not entirely convincing. She opposed his analysis of capitalist development in detail, accusing him of abandoning Marxism and consequently socialism itself, and of being an opportunist. But her argument was internal and circular: Marx's socialism was scientific, not a utopian dream; therefore capitalism was destined to collapse; therefore, there would be socialism. Reality could not survive in the face of the idea. But it is difficult, in retrospect, to fault Bernstein's main observations. Indeed, a decade later Luxemburg herself had to come up with a further explanation for capitalism's continuing survival, which, had she lived, would have had to be followed by another and another.

The SPD and Marxism

The SPD was outlawed by the Nazis in 1933, maintaining an existence in exile. The party was re-established in 1945 but in the Soviet-occupied zone of Germany was forcibly merged with the Communist Party to form the Socialist Unity Party. The SPD in West Germany formally abandoned Marxism in 1959, adopting the Godesburg Programme, which declared the party to be of the people as a whole rather than the working class and to be a supporter of the market system. In 1966 the SPD entered into a coalition with the Christian Democrats and in 1969 formed its first post-war government in alliance with the Free Democrats. At reunification of Germany in 1990 the eastern and western wings of the SPD re-united.

There have been crises, generating two devastating world wars and any number of minor and major depressions, but capitalism as a system – for all the brutality and absurdity vividly and accurately identified by Marx, Luxemburg and others – has triumphed, dominating the 21st century world. The question of collapse remains unanswered.

Luxemburg's major concern was the implication of Bernstein's revisionism for the SPD's *raison d'être*. For the SPD to abandon its faith in capitalism's collapse (and it was a faith for all the claims of 'scientific socialism') would be as if the Roman Catholic Church renounced Christ's resurrection. Why not simply have a party of liberal reform? Luxemburg's dilemma, as she was forced to learn, was that she provided a radical cover for party leaders and theoreticians who, while distancing themselves from Bernstein, would follow him to the letter.

The tension and excitement of the argument exhausted Luxemburg and she stayed in bed for a week after completing the articles for the *Leipziger Volkszeitung*. But rather than congratulating her on what many agreed was a triumph, Jogiches wrote to complain that she had been spending money without consulting him. Luxemburg answered bluntly, *If I'm independent enough to perform single-handed on the political scene, that independence must extend to buying a jacket.*[61] Jogiches's real grievance was Luxemburg's having accepted against his advice an offer to become editor of the SPD newspaper *Sächsiche Arbeiterzeitung*. The authorities in Saxony had expelled Parvus-Helphand and Marchlewski, the paper's joint editors and both non-Germans. They recommended Luxemburg, like them on the party's left, as their successor. She took up her duties at once but the paper's writers, accustomed to a loose rein, objected to editorial direction, particularly from a woman. Luxemburg resigned in November, worn down by endless bickering. One patron, the party chairman August Bebel, wrote to another, Bruno Schönlank, 'I am especially annoyed that she has proved herself too much of a woman and not sufficiently a party comrade. I am disillusioned with her.'[62]

Meanwhile, the debate over revisionism rolled on, moving in October to the SPD congress. Jogiches joined Luxemburg in Stuttgart, but played no part in proceedings. He reluctantly agreed that Luxemburg could reveal their relationship to her family, provided she referred to him as Leo Grozowski. The congress delegates rejected Bernstein's revisionism but criticised Luxemburg and Parvus-Helphand for using over-forceful language in their attacks. Reproached as an upstart newcomer, Luxemburg retaliated sharply, *I know quite well that I still have to win my spurs in the German movement, but I intend to do so on the left wing of the party where they fight the enemy, and not on the right where they compromise with him.* A speaker from the party's 'practical' wing, questioned whether radicals like Luxemburg and Parvus-Helphand were capable of winning votes, which he saw as the party's purpose. 'The pair of them are quite welcome to sit at their desks and expound and elucidate scientific principles. It is we, who have to fight and who have to answer to present and future generations, who should be left to determine our tactics.'[63]

A debate in Stuttgart on the role of women in the party brought Clara Zetkin into Luxemburg's life, beginning a political comradeship and intimate friendship that would last for two decades.

Zetkin, the left-wing editor of *Die Gleichheit*, the SPD women's paper, had already praised 'the valiant Rosa, who pummels that flour-sack Bernstein so vigorously that clouds of powder rise into the air'.[64] At the congress, Zetkin criticised the party's main organ, *Vörwarts*, for its neglect of women's issues. Auer, the SPD secretary, who had despatched Luxemburg to Silesia in June, amused the audience by asking, 'If that is the oppressed sex, then what on earth will happen when they are free and enjoy equal rights?'[65]

When Luxemburg first arrived in Germany, Bebel – who had published the influential *Women and Socialism* in 1878 – had been put out by her lack of interest in the women's movement. She told Jogiches, *When I said that in this matter I can do nothing, and understand nothing, he looked astonished.*[66] Luxemburg was personally reluctant to attach herself to what were seen, in an overwhelmingly men's party, as women's issues, which she feared would be used to

Clara Zetkin (née Eissner) (1857–1933)

Born in Saxony, Zetkin became a socialist and feminist while training as a teacher. She went into exile in Zurich and Paris with her partner Ossip Zetkin in 1882. On her return she became editor in 1891 of the SPD women's paper *Die Gleichheit* (Equality), a position she held until 1917. In 1907 she became head of the party's women's office and in 1911 established the first International Women's Day. She joined the anti-war International Group (later the Spartacist League) in 1914, organised a women's anti-war conference in 1915, and was arrested a number of times. Joining the newly-formed Communist Party in 1919, she was a Reichstag deputy from 1920–33, when she went into exile in the Soviet Union.

keep her away from what she saw as more significant matters. Like men, she saw them as of lesser importance. Greeted by a women's demonstration on her release from prison several years later, Luxemburg, perhaps ironically, complained, *The women would be better occupied mending their husbands' socks and doing the housekeeping.*[67] While Luxemburg was at one with Zetkin politically and there was a genuine affection between them, she had little respect for Zetkin's intellect, describing her on first acquaintance as *a sincere and worthy woman, but also something of an empty piece of rubber hosing.*[68]

In 1892, Zetkin had written, 'The liberation of women workers does not consist merely in obtaining equality with the male world within present society. Rather, the existing social order must be abolished in its entirety, for the economic and property relations of this society are the root of both class and sexual slavery.'[69] Luxemburg agreed entirely, writing two decades later, *Proletarian women, the poorest of the poor, the most disempowered of the disempowered, hurry to join the struggle for the emancipation of women and humankind from the horrors of capitalist domination. Social Democracy has assigned to you a place of honour.*[70] But in the SPD itself, Luxemburg regarded her own and any woman's sex as irrelevant, dismissing the socialist women's movement as *old ladies' nonsense.*[71] She was contemptuous of the concerns of what she scorned as 'bourgeois feminists' and their ambition to find a place for themselves within capitalism. *Most of those bourgeois women who act like lionesses in the struggle against 'male prerogatives' would trot like docile lambs in the camp of conservative and clerical reaction if they had the suffrage ... They are the parasites of the parasites of the social body.*[72] The irony was that both Luxemburg – who arguably was a bourgeois, and remained so in her tastes – and Zetkin, a schoolteacher's daughter, persuaded themselves that taking up Marxism transformed them into proletarians.

Luxemburg did not deny the need for reforms to address women's needs, but insisted they were for socialists – women and men – to win through agitation. The 'minimum programme' of her and Jogiches's SDKPiL, which she had drafted, specifically demanded political equality and the abolition of all laws limiting women's freedom but – as in every other activity – as a means, not an end. Luxemburg wrote of the fight for the vote, *The current mass struggle for women's political rights is only an expression and a part of the proletariat's general struggle for liberation*.[73] She did, however, attack the Belgian socialists in 1903 for dropping their demand for women's suffrage as the price of a coalition with liberals. When the SPD dissolved separate women's organisations in 1908, integrating them into the party structure on the basis that working class unity was paramount, Zetkin nevertheless called for women-only groups, under the control of the party's female members, to be retained for agitation and education. Instead, women – now allowed by law to join the party – were increasingly marginalised, pushed into concentration on what were seen as natural female issues, welfare and children, issues which Luxemburg meticulously avoided.

∾

Luxemburg continued to write for other SPD papers after leaving the *Sächsiche Arbeiterzeitung* in November 1898, but what she earned was never sufficient for her needs. In December she wrote to Jogiches thanking him for 80 marks he had sent, promising it would be the last money she begged. She told him both Kautsky and Franz Mehring, another prominent party intellectual, had asked if she was planning a major opus. But, the excitement over Bernstein subsiding, she told a friend in Switzerland she felt isolated in Berlin, occasionally seeing only the Kautskys, the Bebels and the Mehrings. Jogiches had encouraged Luxemburg's friendship with Kautsky, the leading theoretician of European socialism. Kautsky welcomed Luxemburg as a fellow Marxist of which, he once told her, there were few in the party. As the friendship developed,

Luxemburg spent more time at the Kautskys' home. Luise Kautsky described a division of labour, Luxemburg first discussing politics with her husband, then 'with me everything that makes life more beautiful'. Luise Kautsky knew a Luxemburg who, far from being withdrawn, sang happily in the street, 'arias from Figaro, or songs by Hugo Wolf, or the Marseillaise or the Internationale'.[74]

Luxemburg was regularly at the Kautskys' exclusive 'at homes', where the elite of the German Marxist intelligentsia gathered every Sunday evening. She may have seen the paradox of revolutionaries, enemies of the state, living prosperous bourgeois lives in comfortable houses on fees from the party, with private education for their children and leisurely summer holidays abroad. But – as her letters to Jogiches showed – it was an existence she longed for. In May 1899 she told Jogiches that real influence in the party lay behind the scenes and for the moment she remained outside the charmed circle. *I knew all that in advance, just as I know that within a year or two none of this will matter – the intrigues, the fears, the venom. I shall occupy a position at the top of the party.*[75] It was a remarkable boast for a woman who had been in Germany little over a year, all the more so in the light of remarks of some of her comrades. Luxemburg later told Jogiches she had been called 'an uprooted Jew' and 'a cantankerous woman'. *And please, my love, don't ever advise me to write volumes in self-defence, One may do it in three words or, best, not at all.*[76]

Jogiches continued to resist Luxemburg's pleas to join her in Berlin, pretending now he was studying for his doctorate. Luxemburg believed him, but on 6 March 1899 she wrote a heart-rending reply to a mild hint he had given that they would soon be together. *Oh, Dyodyo, my golden one, if only you keep your promise! … Our own small apartment, our own nice furniture, our own library; quiet and regular work, walks together, an opera from time to time, a small, very small, circle of friends who can sometimes be invited for dinner; every year a summer vacation in the country, one month with absolutely no work! ... And perhaps even a little, a very little baby! Will this never be allowed?* She had seen a child while walking in the Tiergarten, *three or four years old, blond, in a pretty little dress, and staring at me. A compulsion swelled in me to kidnap the child, to dash home and keep it for my own. Oh, Dyodyo, won't I ever have my own baby?*[77] Luxemburg would never have a baby and had to take comfort in a small dog, a rabbit, and then a cat, describing herself as their 'mama'.

Without Jogiches, Luxemburg had an almost independent life, earning an income (but not a living) from her journalism, broadening her scope beyond Polish politics. Once she mocked her ability, writing, *Poor is the party in which a botcher, an ignoramus like me plays an important role.*[78] In June 1899 she contributed an article to the *Leipziger Volkszeitung* criticising the French Socialists for entering a coalition government, implicitly challenging the similar ambitions of the SPD right wing. *In bourgeois society Social Democracy by its very nature is prescribed the role of an opposition party; it may appear as a ruling party only on the ruins of that bourgeois state.*[79] In September she refused the offer of an editorial post on *Vörwarts* on the advice of Bebel, who − mindful of Luxemburg's record on the *Sächsische Arbeiterzeitung* − said there would only be arguments that would end in her storming out.

In April 1900 Luxemburg gave Jogiches an ultimatum, saying she found her position abnormal and humiliating. She had lied to her family, who knew nothing about her marriage in 1898 to Lübeck, pretending she and Jogiches (or Grozowski, as they knew him) had gone through a wedding ceremony in Switzerland. In what sounded like praise for conventionally manipulative relationships between the sexes, Luxemburg told Jogiches, *Here in Berlin I constantly see the kind of women men live with, how those men worship them and yield to their domination, and all the time, in the back of my mind, I am aware of the way you treat me.*[80] After months of prevarication, in August Jogiches relented. He took a room at the house where Luxemburg lived, maintaining his habitual sense of mysterious self-importance by masquerading as her cousin.

Luxemburg's father died in Warsaw in September. She had seen him briefly for a holiday the previous year, their first time together for a decade. Luxemburg only learnt of his death on her return to Berlin from the Socialist International congress in Paris. A few months before, hurt that his daughter never replied to his letters, he had promised not to write again as she was obviously too busy to take any interest. Luxemburg wrote to Kautsky's mother about the impact of her father's death. *This blow shook me so deeply that I could not communicate for many months either by letter or word of mouth.*[81] Much later Luxemburg advised a friend to stay close to his sick father. *I wasn't lucky enough even to have done as little as that. After all, I constantly had to look after the urgent business of humanity and make the world a better place.*[82]

With Jogiches now in Berlin, his idleness – supported by his family's money – was all too obvious. Luxemburg described his inactivity more than once as 'suicidal'. Their life together was not the one she had fantasised about. He had long given up even the pretence of study. The SDKPiL, which he claimed to be directing from exile, was barely functioning and whatever activity there was in Poland was a burden shouldered by Dzierzynski. As Luxemburg busied herself writing, Jogiches brooded alone in his room, his failure emphasized by her success. He avoided the friends who were allowed to know of his existence, having little to contribute to their conversations. Luise Kautsky described Jogiches (whom she knew as Leo Tyschko) ironically as the 'shy conspirator'. In the autumn of 1901 he followed Luxemburg when she moved to a flat at 58 Cranachstrasse in the Friedenau district, where she sublet him a room. Luxemburg took a step closer to the Kautskys' style of life, engaging a maid, Anna, who slept in the kitchen. *I trained her into a model servant*, Luxemburg boasted.[83]

In December 1901 Jogiches's brother Osip arrived in Berlin

from Lithuania in the final stages of tuberculosis. Doctors advised him to seek a warmer climate. Osip left for Algiers, accompanied by Jogiches, who did not return to Germany for almost a year, relieved to escape from an intimacy that was not to his taste. With Jogiches away, Luxemburg was able to enjoy a social life with the SPD elite she had hoped to share with him. Over Christmas she gave two dinners, one for the Kautskys and Eisners, another for the Mehrings and Zetkin. The Kautskys and Eisners came again in the New Year and on 28 January 1902 Luxemburg wrote to Jogiches, *Next Sunday, I'll be going over to the Eisners with Clara, the same night that we're invited to the Kautskys, who are having the Bebels over too.* She went on to describe a party meeting she had spoken at. The best seats at the front, she said, were *naturally taken by Russians or rather by kikes from Russia – they were sickening to look at.*[84] This anti-Semitic note was a revealing reflection of Luxemburg's rejection of her Jewishness.

But Marx, you know, ends up by making me angry 1902–04

In February 1902 the *Leipziger Volkszeitung* offered Luxemburg a post as a contributing editor under her fellow left-winger Mehring. Luxemburg explained excitedly to Jogiches in Algiers on 20 February what the offer meant. *First, loads of money. We could live care-free, spend summers in Switzerland or at the seaside, dress decently, buy things for the apartment (help our folks – this is my special concern …), save several hundred marks every month.* More importantly, she said, it was a permanent political position, a powerful weapon in her pursuit of influence.[85] In March Luxemburg told Clara Zetkin that she and Mehring did much as they wanted, with little interference from the local party's editorial board.

But co-operation was never one of Luxemburg's strengths and over the summer she and Mehring clashed repeatedly. Mehring complained to Kautsky about 'the lady Luxemburg's power complex, her dirty power-grabbing attitude'.[86] She protested that Mehring had cut an article on Poland without consulting her, accusing him of *a deliberate provocation which is but one link in a whole chain of slights.*[87] In October she left the paper. Bebel, a patron since her arrival in Germany, warned Luxemburg that unless she acted more carefully she would find herself isolated from the left as well as the right of the party. She replied that, despite the unfriendly reception she had received in Germany, *It never occurred to me, quite apart from any question of sulking, to withdraw into the corner of scientific*

Rosa Luxemburg *circa* 1904.

study, which is more agreeable and quiet. She had always stuck her neck out and would continue to do so.[88] But for the moment only Kautsky's *Die Neue Zeit* was prepared to provide a platform for her writing, which, to suit the journal's needs, was theoretical rather than agitational.

Jogiches had returned to Luxemburg's Berlin flat in August 1902. Their party, the SDKPiL, revived and Jogiches, roused once more to action, supervised the party's publications, *Red Banner* and *Social Democratic Review*, using the alias Jan Tyszka. The SDKPiL was insignificant beside the more popular nationalist Polish Socialist Party (PPS), but this was beside the point. The objective now was to secure influence in the Russian Social Democratic Labour Party. Luxemburg and Jogiches began producing a newspaper, the *People's Gazette*, intent on undermining the PPS in German Poland. Luxemburg wrote the bulk of the content, as well as supervising printing and distribution. Jogiches wrote nothing himself but complained persistently to Luxemburg about the paper's quality. With a minimal circulation, the *People's Gazette* folded in 1904. But not before Luxemburg had used its pages to energetically abuse delegates to an international women's congress in Berlin, calling them ladies of the bourgeoisie who, *bored with the role of doll or husband's cook, seek some action to fill their empty heads and empty existence.*[89]

Bebel's warning apart, Luxemburg could feel satisfied that she was making progress in her career. In 1903 the International Socialist Bureau – the Socialist International's policy-making body – invited her to become its first woman member. Regional parties continued to invite her to address them, anxious to see and hear Bernstein's nemesis. As in 1898, the party deployed her in Upper Silesia, German-occupied Poland, to rouse voters for the January 1903 Reichstag elections. Straining to be uncontroversial, Luxemburg let slip one critical remark about the Kaiser in a speech. The SPD emerged from the elections as the second force in the Reichstag behind the Catholic Centre Party, increasing its tally from 56 seats to 81. In the aftermath of the elections, Bernstein re-opened conflict by proposing the party should assert its right to provide one of the Reichstag vice-presidents, overturning the SPD's policy of refusing any state office. The party congress in Dresden rejected his suggestion.

The Russian Social Democratic Labour Party (RSDLP) had been formed in 1898. As the SDKPiL's policy was unity of the Polish and Russian workers against tsarism, Luxemburg and Jogiches were keen to play a part in the RSDLP. For the moment, the only issue dividing the two parties was the question of Polish independence, which the SDKPiL opposed and the RSDLP supported. Considering her objective, Luxemburg's actions were paradoxical. When the Russian party congress met in August 1903, first in Brussels (where it was expelled by the Belgian police) and then in London, the SDKPiL's delegates – instructed by Luxemburg – twice walked out of debates on national self-determination.

Theoretical arguments over nationalism were as nothing compared to divisions within the Russian party itself, which Luxemburg became involved in from another direction. In 1902 Vladimir Lenin, a leading figure in the RSDLP, had written *What Is To Be Done* in response to what he saw as a growth of revisionism in the party. In the course of the article he suggested the working class was incapable of arriving at the idea of socialism itself. 'It could only be brought to them from without,' he said. 'The history of all countries shows that the working class exclusively by its own effort, is able to develop only trade union consciousness ... The theory of socialism, however, grew out of the philosophic, historical and economic theories that were elaborated by the educated representatives of the propertied classes, the intellectuals ... The founders of modern scientific socialism, Marx and Engels, themselves belonged to the bourgeois intelligentsia.'[90]

Lenin's conclusion was that to retain the necessary theoretical rigour a Marxist party needed to be centralised, tightly disciplined and made up of professional full-time revolutionaries. Others in the RSDLP, led by Julius Martov, disagreed, arguing that a loose and flexible mass party would be better able to draw in the working class. The RSDLP divided at the 1903 congress, Lenin's supporters taking the name Bolsheviks (from the Russian for 'majority') and Martov's Mensheviks ('minority'). The division, as Trotsky once described it, was between the 'hard' (the Bolsheviks) and the 'soft'. It seemed at first the split could be mended but by 1912 it had become irrevocable. In 1904 the Mensheviks, who controlled the party's paper *Iskra*, asked Luxemburg – as the Socialist International's specialist on Polish and Russian affairs – to analyse the division in the light of a further article Lenin had written, *One Step Forward, Two Steps Back*. Luxemburg's comments – published as *Organisational Questions of Russian Social Democracy* – appeared simultaneously in *Iskra* and *Die Neue Zeit* in July 1904. The Mensheviks were delighted with her contribution. 'Her article will, we hope,' they said in an introduction, 'make clear to comrade Lenin that his stand on organisation has nothing in common with revolutionary Marxism.'[91]

Luxemburg began by acknowledging that organisation was easier in Germany than Russia: Russia was a largely peasant society living under an autocracy, Germany an advanced industrial state with at least the rudiments of bourgeois democracy. But she disagreed fundamentally with the ultra-centralism Lenin had advocated in *One Step Forward, Two Steps Back*. Of course socialist political organisation required centralisation, she said, but it also demanded independent direct action by the masses. *From this it follows that social democratic centralisation cannot be based either in blind obedience or on the mechanical submission of the party's militants to their central authority ...*[92]

Lenin had said he could see no difficulty for the workers in a tightly-controlled party because they were accustomed to the discipline of the factory. Luxemburg dismissed this angrily. *The 'discipline' that Lenin has in mind is instilled in the proletariat not just by the factory but by also by the barracks and by modern bureaucracy – in a word, by the entire mechanism of the bourgeois state ... It is not through the discipline instilled in the proletariat by the capitalist state, with the straightforward transfer of the baton from the bourgeoisie to a social democratic Central Committee, but only the defying and uprooting this spirit of servile discipline that the proletarian can be educated for the new discipline, the voluntary self-discipline of social democracy.*[93] Socialist consciousness was not something party leaders invented and then inserted into the working class; it arose directly from the workers' experience in their spontaneous class struggle.

Lenin's ultra-centralism was, Luxemburg said, *imbued with the sterile spirit of the nightwatchman state.* He feared that intellectuals would seize the workers' movement and mislead it to further their own careers. Luxemburg mocked this, as well she might – one intellectual sparring with another. *In fact nothing will more easily and more surely deliver up a still young proletarian movement to the power-hungry intellectuals than forcing the movement into the strait-jacket of a bureaucratic centralism that reduces the militant workers to a docile instrument of a 'committee'.* She concluded, *Frankly, let us speak between ourselves: the mistakes that are made by a truly revolutionary workers' movement are, historically speaking, immeasurably more fruitful than the infallibility of the best possible 'Central Committee'.*[94]

What Luxemburg left unsaid was that *What Is To Be Done* was no more than Lenin's adaptation to Russian conditions of the thoughts of Kautsky, Luxemburg's ally on the left in the SPD. *One Step Forwards, Two Steps Back* followed logically. Kautsky had written, 'Modern socialist consciousness can arise only on the basis of profound scientific knowledge. The vehicle of science is not the proletariat, but the bourgeois intelligentsia.'[95] In attacking Lenin, Luxemburg was taunting the 'Pope of Marxism', with implications neither would be able to ignore. Kautsky did not publish Lenin's response to Luxemburg in *Die Neue Zeit*. Trotsky, who had taken the Mensheviks' side in the RSDLP split, made similar criticisms of Lenin's views, predicting that power would drift inexorably

A police photograph of Lenin taken in 1905.

from the working class to the party leadership, then into the hands of a single dictator.

Luxemburg's criticisms of Lenin had been typically sparkling, but were they consistent? Her own SDKPiL, limited though it was in scope, operated underground in occupied Poland. One Marxist writer observed that at the moment Luxemburg was attacking Lenin, she, Jogiches and Dzierzynski were attempting to centralise the SDKPiL 'and conducting faction fights against minorities at least in the same (if not more) "harsh" manner as Lenin.'[96] Luxemburg expelled SDKPiL members who disagreed with her, on the basis, it must be assumed, that as a professional intellectual she knew best. Jogiches – with her support – would go further, expelling the entire Warsaw branch in 1912.

A Polish contemporary of Luxemburg, Jan Machajski, posed questions about Marxism going beyond a dispute over organisation to the heart of its ideology. Born in 1866, Machajski's early life had followed a similar pattern to Luxemburg's: study in Warsaw and Zurich, a commitment to Marxism. His activities led to exile in 1892 to Siberia, where he studied Marx's writings more closely. Machajski concluded that 'scientific socialism' was the theory of a new class of intellectuals that had appeared with industrial capitalism. Their objective, conscious or unconscious, was to use the working class to overthrow capitalism and replace the bourgeoisie as rulers. The workers would remain workers, exploited now by an intelligentsia that considered itself entitled to power not because it owned the means of production but because of its superior understanding of the laws of history.[97] As one group of intellectuals argued with another over who most truly represented the working class, there was something impressive about what Machajski said.

Luxemburg understood the danger Machajski outlined, though she did not believe that Marxism had to be the property of intellectuals by right. In her criticism of Bernstein's revisionism she had written, *As long as theoretical knowledge remains the privilege of a handful of 'intellectuals' in the party, it will face the danger of going astray. Only when the great mass of workers has taken into their own hands the keen and dependable weapon of scientific socialism will all the petty-bourgeois inclinations, all the opportunistic currents come to naught.*[98] But what did Luxemburg mean by socialism? No Marxist was expected to describe the society that would replace capitalism in any detail. To do so would be to fall into the utopian fantasising that Marx's 'scientific socialism' was intended to supersede. Marx described how capitalism worked, not socialism and had only momentarily let slip his vision of a post-revolutionary society. But Luxemburg was prepared in 1918 at least to outline a vision of the transition, her Marxism influenced by events in Russia in 1905 and 1917 and the spontaneous emergence of workers' councils in Germany at the end of the First World War.

Capitalism, Luxemburg said, enriched a small number of idlers at the expense of the working class, who, though they produced society's wealth, survived on a meagre wage. Taking hold of the state, and ridding society of the capitalist and the private employer, the working class would transform the economy. *The first duty of a real workers' government is to declare by means of a series of decrees the most important means of production to be national property and place them under the control of society.* Production and distribution would be planned in the common interest. *The essence of socialist society consists in the fact that the great labouring mass ceases to be a dominated mass, but rather, makes the entire political and economic life its own and gives that life a conscious, free, and autonomous direction.*[99]

Workers in every industrial and agricultural enterprise would elect councils. These, in co-ordination with workers' councils in the locality, would order the enterprise's internal affairs, regulate working conditions and control production. But each enterprise would also have managers, Luxemburg said, *who know exactly what they are doing and give the directives so that everything runs smoothly and the best division of labour and the highest efficiency is achieved ... Now it is a matter of willingly following these orders in full, of maintaining discipline and order, of not causing difficulties or confusion.*[100] She did not say who would appoint the managers and whether they would be answerable to the workers' council.

Work would be a social duty, with exemption only for children, the elderly and the sick. Working conditions would be healthier and safer and working hours shorter. The weapons and munitions industries would be dismantled *since a socialist society does not need murder weapons and, instead, the valuable materials and human labour used in them must be employed for useful products. Luxury industries which make all kinds of frippery for the idle rich must also be abolished, along with personal servants.* Productivity would rise under socialism. *The land must yield a far greater crop, the most advanced technology must be used in the factories, only the most productive coal and ore mines must be exploited, etc. It follows from this that socialisation will above all extend to the large enterprises in industry and agriculture.*[101]

A new breed of men and women would be required to construct the new society. *One cannot realise socialism with lazy, frivolous, egoistic, thoughtless and indifferent human beings. A socialist society needs human beings from whom each one in his place is full of passion and enthusiasm for the general well-being, full of self-sacrifice and sympathy for his fellow human beings, full of courage and tenacity in order to dare to attempt the most difficult.* Each worker would *show that he can work hard and properly, keep discipline and give his best without the whip of hunger and without the capitalist and his slave-driver behind him. This calls for inner self-discipline, intellectual maturity, moral ardour, a sense of dignity and responsibility, a complete inner rebirth of the proletarian.*[102]

Legislative and executive power would be exercised by an executive council, elected by a central council of delegates from local workers' councils. The central council would oversee the executive council's actions, with delegates newly elected each time. The local workers' councils would have the right to recall their delegates if they found they were acting against their constituents' interests. The workers' councils would be elected directly in the enterprises and localities, interlinking their activities. Luxemburg had opposed Lenin's conception of the party, sensing that the rigid centralised hierarchy he advocated would carry over into a new society. It is impossible to tell how far as a Communist leader (as Luxemburg briefly was before her death) she would have acted differently. There is nothing in her description of socialism to say what the party and its leaders would be doing after the revolution.

Luxemburg wrote, *The Spartacus League* [the forerunner of the German Communist Party] *will never take over governmental power except in response to the clear, unambiguous will of the great majority of the proletarian mass of all of Germany, never except by the proletariat's conscious affirmation of the views, aims, and methods of struggle of the Spartacus League.*[103] She described a state based on the workers' councils, 'All power to the soviets,' as Lenin would also urge in 1917, before proceeding to smother them. But what role did Luxemburg believe the party would play if the councils were organising society? In a dispute, who would have supremacy, the party or the workers? Luxemburg wrote, *The victory of the Spartacus League ... is identical with the victory of the great million-strong masses of the socialist proletariat.*[104] The argument hung in the air: the party at all times represented the workers' true interests, whether or not they realised it.

After a week's speaking tour in Upper Silesia, followed by a holiday in the Brandenburg Forest, in August 1904 Luxemburg travelled to the Socialist International congress in Amsterdam, one of over 400 delegates from 24 countries. She had credentials from both the German and Polish parties. The congress was notable for the French radical Jean Jaurès's attack on the SPD, which he accused of confusing the workers with ideological complexities. Urging socialist parties to enter coalition governments with liberals, Jaurès declared, 'You do not know yet, in practice, what road you shall take, whether you shall be revolutionary or parliamentary, or how you will institute democracy in your own country.' When he sat down there was no official interpreter to translate his speech into German. Luxemburg, who rejected Jaurès's prescription, although she would have agreed with many of his criticisms of the SPD, stood and repeated what he had said word-for-word in German. Thanking her profusely, Jaurès told the delegates, 'Comrades, you have now seen that infighting is not always a hindrance to co-operation.'[105]

On her return to Berlin in late August, Luxemburg faced a court for her comment about the Kaiser during the previous year's election campaign: *Any man who talks about the good and secure living of the German workers has no idea of the real facts.*[106] The remark was enough to secure her three months in Berlin-Zwickau prison. Though the loss of liberty was punishment enough, conditions were relatively mild. Prisoners could have clothes, papers and books sent in – though Luxemburg was denied a copy of *The Communist Manifesto* – and a party well-wisher paid for meals to be delivered by a local restaurant. She rose at 6 a.m., read, wrote and walked in the yard, going to bed at 9 p.m.

Writing to Jogiches a week into her sentence, Luxemburg asked if he was keeping his promise to read a book a day, as she was. She said a serious book soothed the nervous system. *But Marx, you know, ends up by making me angry. I still can't get the better of him. I keep getting swamped and can't catch my breath.* At the end of the month she criticised Jogiches for his solitary life, which she said was *insane and abnormal, and I take a very dim view of it ... Here I keep grasping greedily at each spark of life, each glimmer of life ... I promise myself to live life to its fullest as soon as I am free.*[107] Luxemburg was released a month early, on 24 October, in a general amnesty following the death of King Albert of Saxony, much to her republican annoyance. On 1 September she had written to Kautsky from her cell, *The interest of the masses is on the move; I feel it even here penetrating through the prison walls.*[108]

The revolution is magnificent. All else is bilge 1904–06

In February 1904, Tsar Nicholas II of Russia declared war on Japan, hoping in part to divert popular attention from mounting domestic problems. When the war ended in June 1905, Russia's ruling class had been humiliated, its armed forces shattered on land and sea, the incompetence and corruption of the regime exposed to the world. In July 1904 Social Revolutionary terrorists had assassinated the Interior Minister Viacheslav Plehve as, after initial enthusiasm, unhappiness with the war and tsarism intensified. In December 1904 workers in St Petersburg struck over the dismissal of members of the Assembly of Russian Factory Workers, a moderate and non-political union founded by an Orthodox priest, Father Georgi Gapon. Within days the strike had spread across the city.

On 22 January 1905 Father Gapon led a workers' deputation to the Tsar's Winter Palace bearing a petition calling for an end to the war, an improvement in factory conditions and civil liberties. The demonstrators sang hymns and carried portraits of the Tsar, but soldiers opened fire on the crowd, killing and wounding hundreds. 'Bloody Sunday' marked the opening of the first stage of the 1905 Russian Revolution. Workers in the city left the factories and workshops in a general strike to protest against the massacre. On 4 February Social Revolutionaries assassinated the Tsar's uncle, Grand Duke Sergei. A wave of strikes swept across

Russia and occupied Poland as the discontent running through Russian society burst out. The middle class and the professions demanded political reform and a constitutional assembly, women called for equality, and the peasants – the majority of the population – formed an All-Russian Peasant Union. In June 1905 a mutiny on the battleship *Potemkin* triggered further defiance in the army and navy.

The government seemed incapable either of repressing the revolt or meeting the variety of demands thrown up by the revolution. On 6 August the Interior Minister Alexander Bulygin proposed a consultative national assembly, with a franchise that denied most workers and peasants a voice. Dissatisfaction with this limited concession provoked a second phase of revolution, with renewed strikes and peasant risings. On 8 October workers on the railway halted all transport, supported by general strikes in the main cities. The Tsar issued a manifesto on 17 October promising a constitution guaranteeing genuine civil liberties. A parliament, the Duma, directly elected on a wider franchise, would have the right to approve or reject legislation.

The working class throughout the Empire, numerically small but geographically concentrated, played a central part in events. The most significant aspect, as Luxemburg would realise, was the revolution's spontaneity, taking socialist parties – the specialists in revolt – by surprise, leaving them in its wake. On 13 October 1905 workers formed a Soviet in St Petersburg, a proletarian parliament made up of directly elected delegates from the factories, trade union representatives and nominees of the radical parties. The Soviet's sympathies seemed closest to the Mensheviks, though the workers showed their irritation with endless theoretical wrangling between them and the Bolsheviks. For six weeks the Soviet wielded greater authority in St Petersburg than the Tsarist government. The mass arrest of members in December provoked an insurrection in Moscow, which was bloodily suppressed, bringing the

Troops about to fire on demonstrators outside the Winter Palace in St Petersburg, 22 January 1905.

high point of the revolution to a close. Revolutionary action was most aggressive in the Empire's non-Russian provinces, Poland in particular. Luxemburg's and Jogiches's SDKPiL had a temporary upsurge in membership. The Russian authorities imposed martial law – lifted after Luxemburg had left Poland in 1889 – in Warsaw in August 1905, extending it nationwide in December.

Luxemburg wrote in *Die Neue Zeit* in late January 1905 that the logic of the 'Bloody Sunday' demonstrators' demands was an end to autocracy. *The humble 'petition' of the masses of the people to the Tsar was in reality nothing but a request that His Sacred Majesty would most graciously condescend with his own hands to decapitate himself as supreme monarch of all the Russians.*[109] Russia, she believed, was not going through a proletarian revolution, but was certainly being pushed towards a bourgeois parliamentary democracy. However, the greater the part the working class played, the stronger their influence would be in whatever state emerged. On 6 February Jogiches left Berlin for Cracow in Austrian-occupied Poland to supervise publication of the SDKPiL's newspaper, *Red Banner*, and to establish an agitational journal, *From the Battlefield*. He smuggled papers and pamphlets into Russian-occupied Poland, crossing the border illegally to Warsaw on five occasions. What impact this had on events is difficult to judge, though Luxemburg herself later admitted that revolutions were not made by propaganda. The local SDKPiL recruited 2,000 members in the midst of the turmoil, only for them to drift away as the excitement subsided.

Luxemburg stayed in Berlin, optimistic, a would-be general way behind the lines. She cancelled a holiday she had planned to take in Holland with the Dutch left-wing socialist Henriette Roland-Holst. *I cannot get away from here. But I feel splendid in my work, for the revolution is growing according to expectations; it is a great joy to watch, understand, and help in its development.*[110] Despite her enthusiasm, and though her letters to Jogiches were full of the tactics to be pressed in *Red Banner*, Luxemburg seemed at times to be detached from events in Russia. In August, without warning, she went to Jogiches in Cracow, where she informed him of her involvement with another man, 'W' as she referred to him in letters, probably a younger SDKPiL member. On 22 August, now back in Berlin, Luxemburg told Jogiches, *You don't want to understand that nothing has changed in my inner relationship with you.* Jogiches returned briefly to Berlin in early September, ostensibly to discuss SDKPiL policy but intent on persuading Luxemburg to end her relationship with W. She appears to have done so, writing to Jogiches on 17 September, *Be strong, Dyodyu, be strong! Now that the worst is over there'll be only peace and energetic work.*[111]

In October, as the second phase of the revolution opened, Luxemburg wrote to Jogiches regretting the impact her political career had had on her family. She said she had cried as she read through her parents' last letters. *I never had time for them because of those world-shaking problems (and still nothing has changed) … Yesterday I was almost ready to give up, once and for all, the goddamn politics (or rather the bloody parody of our 'political' life) and let the whole world go to hell. Politics is an inane Baal worship, driving people – victims of their own obsession, of mental rabies – to sacrifice their entire existence.*[112] Luxemburg's letter than changed track to a complaint about her new maid, 'La donna' as she called her, whom she had spent a day instructing and was already considering dismissing.

One writer has remarked on Luxemburg's 'feudal attitude' towards her servants. 'Her domestic staff was subjected to … demands of fastidiousness both in their personal appearance and in their work; breakages raised Rosa Luxemburg to fury and hatred.'[113] Luxemburg was accustomed to servants from childhood, and the upper echelons of the SPD who were her closest friends – the Kautskys, for example – found life impossible without them. Luxemburg's male peers had wives, and their wives had servants. It is possible that Luxemburg's only real contact with the working class may have been through servants and the audiences applauding her speeches. She was never a Reichstag deputy with a constituency to nurse and workers were not in her circle. She once wrote, *Contact with the masses gives me inner courage and tranquillity.*[114] The masses: theorised, the working class as an idea. She was aware of the anomaly employing servants as drudges represented and may sometimes have felt uncomfortable. Under socialism, Luxemburg wrote in 1918, there would be no place for *personal servants. All the human labour tied up there will be found a more worthy and useful occupation.*[115]

⁓

What impressed Luxemburg about events in Russia were the mass, or general, strikes, drawing the workers of a city or region together to press their economic and political demands. In May 1905 the German Free Trade Union congress in Cologne rejected the mass strike as a tactic, fearing the impact on their funds. They were unwilling to see an industrial weapon used to win a political end, interfering in what they saw as the traditional division of labour. Unions won pay increases, parties won votes. Luxemburg was both amused and angry at the union leaders' *self-satisfied, beaming and self-assured narrow-mindedness which was a joy unto itself, intoxicated with itself, and considered itself far above all the experiences of the international working class movement.*[116]

In September 1905 Luxemburg raised the issue at the SPD congress at Jena, urging the party to seriously consider the political mass strike. As speaker after speaker attacked her motion, Luxemburg was exasperated at what she saw as their parochialism, telling the congress, *Anyone listening here to the previous speeches ... must really feel like clutching his head and asking: 'Are we actually living in the year of the glorious Russian Revolution, or are we ten years behind the times?'* She quoted the last lines of *The Communist Manifesto*, asking the delegates whether they understood what Marx and Engels had meant when they wrote, 'The proletarians have nothing to lose but their chains. They have a world to win.' When Luxemburg sat down Bebel remarked, 'Listening to all that, I could not help glancing a couple of times at the toes of my boots to see if they weren't already wading in blood.'[117] The authorities took a similar view, later charging Luxemburg with incitement to violence.

Bebel put a compromise motion forward, suggesting the mass

strike could be used to defend workers' voting rights, which Kautsky and even Bernstein, the left's revisionist adversary, found acceptable. Luxemburg withdrew in favour of Bebel, satisfied to have at least won acceptance for the principle. In February 1906 she discovered the SPD and trade union leadership had reached a secret agreement to ignore the Jena resolution.

On the surface Luxemburg remained influential, a regular contributor to the party's theoretical organ *Die Neue Zeit*, basking in Kautsky's admiration of her intellect, if not always where it led her. Constant vilification by the mainstream press as 'red Rosa' and 'revolutionary Rosa' only enhanced her firebrand reputation. In October 1905, temporarily emboldened by events in Russia, the party executive committee dismissed six associate editors suspected of revisionist sympathies from the SPD daily *Vorwärts*, replacing them with left-wingers, including Luxemburg. She was contemptuous of her new colleagues' abilities, telling Jogiches, *The editorial board is made up of morons, conceited morons to boot. 'Journalist?' – not a single one … If you could just see their style! I want to jump out of my skin! Needless to say, all that is in store for us (that is, radicals) is utter disgrace.*[118]

∽

What interested the German press was why, if Luxemburg was so dedicated to revolution, she did not go to Poland, the land of her birth, and join the uprising? The right-wing *Die Hilfe* asked pointedly, 'What on earth would this gallant lady do in the unlikely event of her speeches and articles really setting off a conflagration in Germany? Would she stick it out here or would she decamp to yet another clime on the international scene?'[119] Luxemburg had been writing articles urging on the revolution, over 90 in the course of 1905, but depended almost entirely on Jogiches for news, invariably second- and third-hand. Jogiches had been enjoying his independence, with a role of his own, working closely with the left wing of the Polish Socialist Party and the Jewish workers movement, the Bund. He supervised the production of leaflets in Polish and Yiddish, and in Russian to influence the occupying army.

At the end of November Jogiches travelled to Warsaw for a meeting with his fellow SDKPiL leaders Marchlewski, Warski and Dzierzynski, registering at a hotel as Otto Engelman. Luxemburg decided to join them. On 28 December 1905 Karl and Luise Kautsky saw her off at Friedrichstrasse station. Hardly an unrecognisable figure – she had been photographed at SPD and Socialist International conferences – Luxemburg travelled as Anna Matschke, using the passport of a Berlin party member. On her arrival in Warsaw, travelling for most of the journey on a Russian troop train, she sent a postcard to the Kautskys. *The city is as quiet as the grave; general strike, soldiers wherever you look. The work is going well; today I begin.*[120]

Luxemburg joined the revolution as it was subsiding, although Russian soldiers were still shooting protestors at banned demonstrations. On 2 January 1906 Luxemburg reported to the Kautskys that the general strike had played itself out. *Now only direct and general street fighting can decide matters, but the right moment for this must still be prepared.*[121] She continued to write articles for the SDKPiL newspaper, but police had raided the printing shop. With romantic exaggeration, Luxemburg told the Kautskys, *Every day, gun in hand, we force the bourgeois printers to print the Banner.*[122] Within a fortnight of her arrival, Luxemburg's health had worsened, but she told the Kautskys she hoped her condition would improve. She visited her brothers and sister once a week, explaining that she was too busy to see them more frequently.

Luxemburg stayed in a pension a few minutes walk from Jogiches's hotel. At the end of February, the revolution over, she was preparing to return to Berlin. Jogiches – inexplicably, given his

Polish police photographs of Rosa Luxemburg taken in 1906.

reputation as a hardened conspirator – moved into the pension a day or two before Luxemburg was due to leave. On 4 March the police raided it and searched her room, where they found illegal literature and letters confirming whatever suspicions they had had. The officers arrested Luxemburg and Jogiches, who both maintained their false identities. Luxemburg was taken to the City Hall and placed with a dozen other prisoners in a cell intended for one. She wrote to the Kautskys, *During the day the cell doors are left open, and we are allowed to walk the whole day in the corridor, to mix with the prostitutes and listen to their lovely ditties and expressions, and to enjoy the odours wafting from the equally wide open lavatories.*[123]

The authorities discovered Luxemburg's true identity and brought her sister, Anna, to identify her. Unmasked, Luxemburg claimed she was in Warsaw representing the SPD press and that she had no involvement in Polish politics. She was transferred to the Warsaw Citadel, where her revolutionary heroes had been executed in 1886. Luxemburg wrote to Luise Kautsky asking the party to keep up the rent on her flat and to pay a tailor's bill for Jogiches. The SPD proposed approaching the Imperial Chancellor,

Carl von Bülow, for help. Luxemburg refused, saying it would seem ungrateful to criticise his policies if she owed her freedom to him. Illness and bribery secured her liberty. Doctors found a multitude of ailments – anaemia, dilation of the liver, hysterical and neurasthenic symptoms and catarrh of the stomach and intestines – that the prison was not equipped to cope with. Luxemburg's family bribed a Russian officer 2,000 roubles to authorise bail, which the SPD guaranteed.

The prison released Luxemburg into the care of her family on 28 June 1906. She told her German socialist friends Mathilde and Emmanuel Wurm on 17 July that they were fortunate to be living in passionate times and that she was itching to write about the mass strikes. *The revolution is splendid. All else is bilge.*[124] After a further examination doctors recommended that Luxemburg should undergo treatment at a spa outside Poland. She left Warsaw on 31 July, still on bail pending trial. She went briefly to St Petersburg, where she visited the imprisoned Parvus-Helphand, and then on to Kuokkala in Finland, where she spent the summer under the alias Felicja Budzilowicz, writing a pamphlet on the events in Russia. Luxemburg renewed her acquaintance with Lenin, their relations untarnished by their clash over party organisation. She wrote to a friend, *It is a pleasure to talk to him. He is sophisticated and knowledgeable, with the kind of ugly mug I like so much.*[125]

Jogiches, meanwhile, kept his real identity from the authorities until the end of June 1906. On 10 January 1907 he faced a court martial for membership of the illegal SDKPiL, attempting to overthrow Tsar Nicholas, and desertion. Luxemburg sent a medical certificate saying she was too ill to attend. Jogiches was sentenced to eight years' hard labour but escaped in April on the eve of his transportation to Siberia.

∼

Luxemburg returned to Berlin from Finland on 13 September 1906 with the completed manuscript of *The Mass Strike, the Political Party, and the Trade Unions*, encapsulating the lessons she was determined Western European socialists should learn from the revolution in Russia. One problem faced her: the spontaneity of the workers' strikes and peasants' risings vindicated the Anarchist view of how revolution erupted and developed rather than the Marxist view. The two strands of left-wing thought had been enemies since the clash between Marx and Bakunin in the First International, libertarianism facing authoritarianism. Defensively, Luxemburg opened the pamphlet with an attack on the Anarchists, distorting their attitude toward the general – or as she had renamed it – mass strike.

Anarchism's return as a rival to Marxism in the working class took the form of anarcho-syndicalism. In 1906 the strongest French trade union organisation, the Conféderation Générale du Travail, had adopted a programme excluding political parties, confident that the workers could organise themselves to overthrow capitalism. In the United States, the Industrial Workers of the World was developing on similar lines and anarcho-syndicalist movements were growing in Spain and Italy. In Germany, SPD members were inviting Anarchists and anarcho-syndicalists to their meetings in the provinces. Luxemburg rejected attempts by the SPD leadership to ban them, telling the Mannheim party congress, *Anarchism in our ranks is nothing else but a left reaction against the excessive demands of the right ... Since we have never kicked out anyone on the far right, we do not now have the right to evict the far left.*[126]

Was Luxemburg's enthusiasm leading her perilously close to Anarchism, or at least a hybrid anarcho-Marxism? The SPD leadership certainly thought so. As she was later to complain, *At every annual party congress the energetic protests of the left wing against the policy of parliamentarism-only ... were stigmatised as anarchism, anarcho-socialism, or at least anti-Marxism.*[127] Luxemburg described in her pamphlet how mass strikes were the most significant aspect of the 1905 revolution, spontaneous, not directed by the parties or trade unions. *If, therefore, the Russian revolution teaches us anything, it teaches above all that the mass strike is not artificially 'made', not 'decided' at random, not 'propagated', but that it is an historical phenomenon which, at a given moment, results from social conditions with historical inevitability.* But, wary of pushing the SPD leadership too far, she painted the mass strike as a new Marxist rather than an old Anarchist tactic. *It is a testimony to the sound revolutionary instinct and to the quick intelligence of the mass of the German proletariat that, in spite of the obstinate resistance of their trade union leaders, they are applying themselves to this new problem with such keen interest.*[128]

Luxemburg vividly outlined the events of what she saw as a glorious year, emphasising the persistent self-organisation of the workers and the flexibility of their tactics. *All these conditions cannot be fulfilled by pamphlets and leaflets, but only by the living political school, by the fight and in the fight, in the continuous course of the revolution.* German trade unionists might fear their organisations would shatter like porcelain in the rage of revolution, but Russia had shown the opposite. *From the whirlwind and the storm, out of the fire and glow of the mass strike and the street fighting rise again, like Venus from the foam, fresh, young, powerful, buoyant trade unions.*[129] Luxemburg neglected one of the most significant developments, the emergence of the workers' council, the Soviet, which she referred to in passing as little more than a strike committee. This was an interesting blind spot in her observations.

If the workers made their own revolution and even – though Luxemburg had not noticed – created their own administration in the form of the workers' councils, what was the party for? Did the workers learn as they went along or did they need to rely on Marxist theoreticians for guidance? There is a tension between the two in *The Mass Strike. Consistent, resolute, progressive tactics on the part of the Social Democrats produces in the masses a feeling of security, self-confidence and desire for struggle; vacillating weak tactics, based on an underestimation of the proletariat, has a crippling and confusing effect upon the masses.*[130] Luxemburg was describing the gulf between what she wanted the SPD to be – daring, stirring, combative – and its reality as a sluggish electoral machine. While the party might not be able to make a revolution, it could in her view hold one back.

Luxemburg sent her family in Warsaw a cutting from an SPD newspaper, evidence of her popularity in the wake of events in Russia. 'If the mere appearance of comrade Luxemburg was greeted by enthusiastic cheers and her statements were often interrupted by stormy applause, the end of her speech was met with a thunderous ovation … Even on the street she was loudly cheered and her way back to the hotel turned into a triumphant procession.'[131] But an awkward element had been introduced in Luxemburg's relations with Kautsky, until now, despite some reservations on her part, an ally on the left. Kautsky believed that what had happened in Russia – sympathetic though he was with a people struggling for democracy – was only to be expected from a backward, barely industrialised society. He considered Germany could learn nothing from it, while Luxemburg saw the SPD as having everything to learn. A decade later, Luxemburg admitted, *The revolution of 1905–07 roused only a faint echo in Europe.*[132] Luise Kautsky recorded that whenever her husband and Luxemburg were together they debated the question. 'Yet, despite the heat of the argument there was never even the suggestion of a breach in their friendship.'[133] Initially perhaps, but the dispute grew bitter as Kautsky felt himself squeezed by the right and battered by Luxemburg from the left.

He wriggles like a cornered snake 1907–12

Elections to the Reichstag in January 1907 were held against the background of growing antagonism between the European powers. Britain, fearing German industrial rivalry and the challenge posed to her naval supremacy, was constructing alliances with France and Russia. Germany was fighting a colonial war in South West Africa (now Namibia), a gift from Britain and France in 1885 as a consolation for arriving late in the race for colonies. The territory's original inhabitants, the Herero, waged a guerrilla war in the three years from 1904 and were ruthlessly suppressed by German troops. Meanwhile, in March 1905 Kaiser Wilhelm II visited Tangier and delivered a clumsy speech supporting Moroccan independence, an open challenge to French dominance in North Africa. The French government, backed by Britain, made warning noises; Germany mobilised reserve army units and France moved men to the frontier. An international conference at Algeçiras in the spring of 1906 relieved, but did not end, the festering tension. Luxemburg had written prophetically to Jogiches in 1899. *It's clear that the dismemberment of Asia and Africa is the limit beyond which European politics no longer has room to unfold ... The European powers will have no choice other than throwing themselves on one another, until the period of the final crisis sets in within politics.*[134]

The Imperial Chancellor, von Bülow, fought the election on a nationalist and militarist platform, rousing voters' fears of enemies abroad and socialists within. The SPD, which until now had shown little interest in overseas affairs, put German colonial brutality in Africa at the centre of its campaign. Luxemburg addressed party meetings, often of two or three thousand, and claimed her audiences asked one question above all, 'Tell us about the Russian revolution.' That may very well have been true among the party rank and file, but liberal middle class voters the party had hoped to woo were persuaded that Germany was in peril and moved to the right. The SPD saw its representation in the Reichstag fall from 81 seats to 43 and, although the party's overall working class vote rose by 300,000, the recriminations began.

The SPD right blamed the left's radical rhetoric for the losses, calling for a period of quiet and an acceptance of the nationalist tide. At Easter Luxemburg accompanied Kautsky on a working holiday to Lake Geneva to formulate the position *Die Neue Zeit* should take to re-assert in the party what they both believed was their shared Marxist view. But Luxemburg found him, as she wrote to a friend, *heavy, dull, unimaginative, ponderous.*[135] Shortly after their return, Luxemburg made a joke revealing her growing disillusionment. It was at one of the Kautskys' Sunday soirées. Luxemburg described how she and Clara Zetkin had wandered onto a military rifle range during a country stroll. Bebel began composing an obituary for the two women but his inspiration faltered. Luxemburg interrupted that it would be enough to say, *Here lie the last two men of German Social Democracy.*[136]

Luxemburg continued the theme in a letter to Zetkin in March. *Since my return from Russia I have felt rather isolated here. I feel the pettiness and indecisiveness which reigns in our party more brutally and more painfully than ever before ... I feel that those masses who are organised in the party are tired of parliamentarism, and would welcome a new line in party tactics, but the party leaders and still more the upper stratum of opportunist editors, deputies and trade union leaders are like an incubus.* But she was confident the situation would change in time. *The tasks are many and I calculate that it should take many years to complete them.*[137]

~

Luxemburg was able to transform her personal life more rapidly. When Jogiches returned to Berlin in April 1907 she told him their relationship was over. He did not know – and probably never would – that he had been replaced in the 36-year-old Luxemburg's affections by Konstantin 'Costia' Zetkin, Clara Zetkin's son. Sensitive and sentimental, the opposite of Jogiches, the 21-year-old Costia had been allowed by the SPD, which was paying the rent, to live in Luxemburg's flat while she was in Poland. On her return Luxemburg let him stay on in what had been Jogiches's room. In the late autumn or early winter of 1906 they became lovers. Their shared tastes for romanticism in music and poetry drew them together, while Luxemburg found Costia's almost total lack of concern for politics refreshing. When Costia finally went back to his mother's home in Stuttgart he was a frequent but discreet visitor to Cranachstrasse.

Jogiches reacted violently to his rejection. Luxemburg wrote to a friend, *The man is emotionally a wreck, he is abnormal and lives all the time with only one fixed idea in mind – to kill me.* She said she had bought a revolver to protect herself. But despite her fear, she felt a sense of liberation. *I am only I, once more, since I have become free of Leo.*[138] The two eventually came to a compromise. Jogiches slept at a hotel in nearby Steglitz (under the alias K Krzysztalowick) but worked at the flat in the day with books they had bought together. Jogiches enjoyed expensive tailoring and the bills continued to arrive at Luxemburg's flat. She tried to create a new life for herself, visiting galleries and concerts with friends who were not obsessed with politics, renewing her interest in painting. Luxemburg produced a self-portrait about this time, describing it

Leo Jogiches photographed *circa* 1906.

as *Ein Klumpen von Lumpen* – an assortment of lumps.[139] She began to read novels again, without Jogiches accusing her of wasting time. Fiction, she told Clara Zetkin, half-excusing herself, was *as necessary as one's daily bread to counteract the desolation of the spirit by the mundane treadmill of trade union and parliamentary struggle and the poverty of our agitation.*[140]

Luxemburg and Jogiches were still leading figures in the SDKPiL. In 1906 the party had fused with the RSDLP, which continued to be racked by the Bolshevik-Menshevik split. Jogiches insisted they both attended the RSDLP congress in London in May 1907. Luxemburg carried delegate's credentials from both the SDKPiL and the German Social Democrats. She wrote to Costia from London that she had hoped the ferry would sink in the English Channel, so fraught had the journey been with Jogiches. In her hotel room, he opened a letter (unsigned, but from Costia) and, accusing her of having a lover, said he would kill them both. At dinner he whispered he would rather kill her than let her return to Germany. Frightening perhaps, but Luxemburg's letter to Costia describing Jogiches's threats bubbled with excitement and a relish for the drama.

Trotsky, who had played a part in the St Petersburg Soviet, left a portrait of Luxemburg as she appeared at the congress. 'She was a little woman, frail, and even sickly looking, but with a noble face, and beautiful eyes that radiated intelligence; she captivated one by the sheer courage of her mind and character.'[141] In her first speech on the evening of 16 May Luxemburg brought greetings from the SPD, telling the delegates revolution was inevitable in Germany 'sooner or later'. She called, on behalf of the SPD central committee, for the Bolsheviks and Mensheviks to heal their quarrel. While she criticised both even-handedly, the former for their belief that alliances could be made with bourgeois liberal parties, the latter for Lenin's mechanistic view of organisation, Luxemburg's sympathies were with the Bolsheviks. Jogiches and Adolf Warski were elected to the RSDLP central committee as Bolshevik allies.

Luxemburg returned to Germany to face trial for incitement to violence. In a speech to the 1906 Jena party congress she had urged the working class to emulate their Russian comrades. Finding the charge proved, the court sentenced her to two months' imprisonment. Costia had now replaced Jogiches at the centre of Luxemburg's dreams for a secure domestic life and she wrote from her cell mapping out their future together. She asked him, as she had Jogiches, to promise that he was studying seriously. Jogiches, meanwhile, reclaimed his old room in Luxemburg's flat.

There was a persistent tension between Luxemburg's admiration for working class spontaneity and her desire for control through a revolutionary vanguard. One aspect of this came out in a speech she made to the International Socialist Women's conference in August 1907. She was describing her work as the only female member of the Brussels-based International Socialist Bureau, the executive committee of the Socialist International. *I must tell you frankly that probably only those comrades who have felt the influence of the International Bureau from afar have such a high admiration of it.*[142] She complained that parties affiliated to the Socialist International ignored the Bureau because it did not have the authority to command them, allowing them to follow their own national interests. This, she believed, did not reflect the internationalism at the heart of socialism. If Luxemburg wanted national parties to be under rigid control, it presupposed that the parties themselves would take an equally rigorous attitude towards their members' actions. It would take war and revolution to create the type of International, the Communist International, in which parties would obey orders from the centre.

The Socialist International's stance on war provided an example of what worried Luxemburg. The Morocco crisis in 1905 showed how little thought socialist parties had given to what they should do collectively if a European war broke out. They debated the issue at the August 1907 Socialist International congress in Stuttgart. The French socialists Jean Jaurès and Edouard Vaillant proposed mass strikes and refusal of military service, even in a defensive war. Bebel, echoing others who feared their governments would seize any opportunity to suppress the socialist movement, put forward a less precise and safer suggestion: socialists in the national parliaments and workers should do whatever was effective to prevent an outbreak of war.

Luxemburg, the Bolshevik Lenin and the Menshevik Martov worked together to give Bebel's resolution a more radical thrust. The socialist parties should, as Bebel said, take every possible action to prevent hostilities but, they added, 'Should war break out nevertheless, it is their duty to advocate its speedy end and to utilise the economic and political crisis brought about by the war to rouse the various social strata and to hasten the overthrow of capitalist rule.'[143] The Socialist International accepted the resolution as a convenient compromise, perhaps relieved at the lack of an explanation of how it would be put into effect. The parties of the Socialist International re-affirmed the resolution in Copenhagen in 1910 and Basle in 1912, but ignored it completely when war came in August 1914.

Rosa Luxemburg speaking at the International Socialist Congress in Stuttgart in 1907.

Running through the issue of war was that of nationalism, which Luxemburg believed Marxists should oppose. Even liberals believed it would be a waning force as capitalism international-ised, or, in contemporary parlance, globalised. Lenin's support for national self-determination was, like Marx's over Poland, a tactical position intended to undermine the European empires. Nevertheless, Luxemburg took him at his word, writing a series of polemical articles for the SDKPiL's *Social Democratic Review*. She attacked Lenin's thinking as out of tune with Marxism, for which there were no eternal truths. *A right of nations which is valid for all countries and at all times is nothing more than a metaphysical cliché of the type of 'rights of man' and 'rights of the citizen'.* The nation had no reality, Luxemburg said, there were only classes and their interests in a capitalist world. *If we find in the history of modern societies 'national' movements, and struggles for 'national' interests, these are usually class movements of the ruling strata of the bourgeoisie ... The Social Democracy is called upon to realise not the right of nations to self-determination but only the right of the working class, which is exploited and oppressed, of the proletariat, to self-determination.*[144] But a well-turned argument would not persuade the bulk of the working class to abandon national sentiment, as Luxemburg learned to her distress in August 1914.

～

Luxemburg's break with Jogiches implied that she would have to earn her own living. Subsidised by Jogiches since their earliest days together, Luxemburg was notorious among her friends for carelessness over money, her own and that of others. She paid tradesmen only reluctantly, allowing bills to mount until they threatened legal action. In October 1907, with fortunate timing, the party school offered Luxemburg a post as tutor. The conditions were generous: 3,000 marks for a term running from October to March, lecturing two hours a day, four days a week, on Marxist economic theory with *Das Kapital* at the centre.

The school had opened in November 1906, with 30 budding party and union administrators and officials attending each annual session. Kautsky had been asked to take the economics class from 1 October 1907 but recommended Luxemburg in his place, writing to the SPD head of education, 'In Rosa Luxemburg you will be getting one of the best brains in Germany.'[145] She accepted and remained on the school's staff until war broke out in 1914. Luise Kautsky had no doubt of Luxemburg's ability. 'She possessed all the prerequisites of a pedagogue: not only was she gifted and thoroughly educated, but she also possessed the self-confidence and self-assurance that a teacher needs to impress ... students.'[146] On Sunday afternoons, Luxemburg emulated the Kautskys' 'at homes' by inviting groups of the most able or interesting students to her flat for tea and discussion.

Jogiches had given Luxemburg some respite by leaving Berlin in September 1907 to work in Finland with the Russian Social

Democrats. He returned in January 1908 to the hotel in Steglitz but seemed unwilling to accept the relationship had finished. He watched and followed Luxemburg, bursting into her flat one night, possibly hoping to find her with a lover. She ran to the Kautskys, who lived a few streets away. When she returned she found Jogiches had rifled through her papers and taken her keys. In the midst of this turmoil, Luxemburg was managing her affair with Costia, taking his life in hand and trying to persuade him into some activity, as she had with Jogiches. An intellectual drifter, still – like many in this circle – living off his family, Costia saw no reason to settle to anything. Luxemburg, infatuated, tried to give him some direction, recommending books to read, suggesting he became a novelist, then a painter, then a sculptor. When Costia drew away, as Jogiches had, her possessiveness grew.

In the summer of 1909, after they had broken and then renewed their relationship, Luxemburg and Costia's mother Clara proposed to Bebel and Kautsky that the party gave him a post at the school. Luxemburg prepared outline lectures for him on West European socialism until Bebel and Kautsky reminded her Costia had no experience and had never showed any sign of commitment to the SPD. After a holiday together in August 1909 the relationship cooled again when Luxemburg suspected Costia was involved with another, younger woman. To retrieve her pride, she wrote saying he had been mistaken all along and that she had wanted no more than friendship. The affair revived briefly, but with none of its previous intensity, and dwindled away.

As a fellow leader of the SDKPiL Luxemburg could not ease Jogiches out of her life so simply. He continued to use her flat as a library but in September 1909 she asked him to leave her in peace and to conduct party business in writing. She said she did not enjoy the sense that anyone could come or go at will and wanted to feel the flat was her own. *If there is no way I can have it, I prefer to give up the whole apartment with the maid and to sublet a furnished room just so I would know that I am living at home, not in a hotel.*[147] But at other times, particularly when the affair with Costia had ended, she wrote telling Jogiches she was lonely, that she was suffering from migraines and depression, and recalled events from their time together. Occasionally she asked for money, disguised as a request to the 'party' rather than Jogiches himself.

~

Despite the setback in the 1907 Reichstag elections, the SPD maintained its strength of organisation. A bureaucracy armed with funds running into hundreds of thousands of marks, a chain of national and regional newspapers, printing works, offices, meeting halls and social clubs throughout Germany staffed by hundreds of officials, building societies, producers' and consumers' co-operatives, all serving over a million paid-up members, reaching out to millions more voters. What concerned Luxemburg and the left was that the SPD leadership, nursing the party as an electoral machine, encouraged the working class to feel they could be comfortable in the capitalist state rather than overthrow it, Bernstein's revisionism winning by default. Luxemburg wrote to a friend, *German party life is nothing but a bad dream, or rather a dreamless leaden sleep.*[148] The dream was about to be broken.

In 1909 Kautsky published *The Road to Power*, confirming Luxemburg's fears that he had accepted the party's direction and bringing their relationship to a crisis. 'Social Democracy,' he wrote, 'is a revolutionary but not a revolution-making party ... It is no part of our work to instigate a revolution or to prepare the way for it.'[149] In the course of a few months the political and personal friendship between Luxemburg and Kautsky – who had welcomed her as a fellow Marxist in 1898 – was shattered in a painfully vicious argument, played out in the party press.

The immediate cause was a proposed reform of the Prussian

electoral system that even conservatives opposed and was subsequently abandoned. Although the reform offered a modification of the three-class voting system, it did not meet SPD demands for an end to the system itself and for a redistribution of seats in favour of the urban areas, where the party had its strength. Political power would remain in the hands of the wealthier classes. In February and March 1910 the SPD led demonstrations against the proposed changes. Luxemburg said this was the time to mount mass strikes to press the party's argument, and the call was taken up by a number of regional party organisations. Trotsky, now living in Germany, met Luxemburg at Kautsky's house before they left to join a protest in Berlin. He found them in the middle of an angry argument about the mass strike as a tactic. 'In Rosa's retorts one could hear suppressed indignation, and in Kautsky's answers one sensed a profound inner embarrassment disguised by rather uncertain jokes,' Trotsky recorded.[150]

Luxemburg described that day's demonstration in a letter to Clara Zetkin. *Of course, the masses, as soon as they see police horses and drawn sabres, beat it without a moment's thought ...* She and others had stood their ground. *Naturally the cops didn't dare touch us; but everything can be learned, including not to run away.* After addressing a meeting two weeks later she wrote to Luise Kautsky, *I unsheathed my sword, and this met with strong applause.* She said party branches all over Germany were inviting her to speak on the mass strike. *I am considering whether I should quit the school and move into the country to fan the fires everywhere.*[151]

Kautsky took the first step in distancing himself from Luxemburg by declining to publish her article, 'What Next?', in *Die Neue Zeit*. He did not object to her calls for mass strikes or even for demonstrations to be organised like military manoeuvres, but found her demand for a republic intolerable. 'Your article is very beautiful and important,' he said in his rejection letter, but a republic was not in the SPD programme. 'A single personality, however high she may stand, cannot pull off a fait accompli on her own hook which can have unforeseeable consequences for the party.'[152] Kautsky's tone suggested Luxemburg had exhausted his patience. The *Dortmunder Arbeiterzeitung* printed the article at the end of the month, with the reference to a republic removed. Luxemburg could have made this compromise with Kautsky, but evidently chose not to. He responded in *Die Neue Zeit* with an article entitled 'What Now?' shifting his criticism to the issue of the mass strike, which he said was not suited to German conditions. It became clear in the course of his article that by revolution he had come to mean winning a majority in the Reichstag.

In April Luxemburg took leave from the party school, as she had told Luise Kautsky she would. In Berlin she roused a meeting of 6,000 party members with her definition of the working class. *We are the millions of those whose work makes society possible … we can show our reactionary rulers once and for all that the world can go on without Junkers and Earls, without councillors and at a pitch even without police; but that it cannot exist for 24 hours if one day the workers withdraw their labour.* In her final rally at Frankfurt-on-Main she faced an audience of 7,000. Nervous, for all her experience as a speaker, she wrote to a friend, *As usual I feel sick at the contact with this coagulated mass of strange people.*[153]

Kautsky had thrown down his challenge to Luxemburg in 'What Now?' while she was on the speaking tour. Angry at Kautsky's unwillingness to confront her directly, Luxemburg wrote to Jogiches that she would be dealing with him. To Luise Kautsky, who had herself been briefly estranged from her husband, she said in a postcard from Dortmund, *With his courageous stab in the back he has really gotten himself into hot water.*[154] The battle intensified between May and August 1910, Kautsky uncomfortable at being vilified from the radical left after having, as he thought, seen off the right in the revisionism debates. In his own mind he had never moved from what now became the 'Marxist centre'.

Unavoidably, the personal and the political were intertwined, as two priests of Marxism, once comrades and friends, accused one another of misinterpreting and then wilfully distorting the holy writ of the founding fathers. In June Kautsky defended his position, posing his 'strategy of attrition' against Luxemburg's 'strategy of overthrow', open confrontation with the state.

Luxemburg retorted with 'Theory and Practice', a step-by-step demolition not only of Kautsky's views but those of orthodox Marxism, which he published, quixotically, in *Die Neue Zeit*. The most effective way to defend existing rights was, she said, to press for new rights, to stay on the offensive. She accused Kautsky of succumbing to nationalist fervour, praising the historical glories of the German state. Against this she posed German imperial adventures in China and the massacres in South West Africa. She said his strategy for socialism amounted to *Nothing-But-Parliamentarism*. Luxemburg worked through Kautsky's previous statements point by point, tying him in knots over his contradictions. No party, she concluded, could hold back the revolution in Germany. *If once the revolutionary period is fully unfolded, if the clouds of battle are already rising high, then no brake-pulling by the party leaders will be able to accomplish much, for the masses will simply shove aside their leaders who set themselves against the storm of the movement.*[155] The future struggle would be waged neither in the Reichstag nor on the barricades, but through mass strikes. Kautsky replied and Luxemburg responded again.

In her exchanges with Kautsky, as in so much of her writing, Luxemburg is not talking to or for the working class, but engaging in a competition of ideas; Bernstein in 1899, Lenin in 1904, now Kautsky. Her style, her rhetoric, is deployed to win an argument against an immediate opponent, another socialist. The game is private, exclusive, academic. Luxemburg felt she was gaining the upper hand over Kautsky, exposing him as a mere theoretician, afraid to dirty his hands with the reality of revolution. On holiday in Switzerland, she boasted in a letter to Jogiches, *He wriggles like a cornered snake.*[156] A few days later Kautsky went into hospital, where he was confined for several months, his nerves shattered. Luxemburg complained to Jogiches that she was being blamed. August Bebel, Luxemburg's earliest patron in Germany, told Luise Kautsky that Luxemburg had brought on her husband's collapse by encouraging the breakdown of their marriage. In 1908 Luise Kautsky had fled to Vienna. She wrote to her husband that she planned to live with his brother Hans, but returned when Kautsky refused to give up custody of their youngest son. Luxemburg was close to Luise Kautsky and, after her break with Jogiches, persistent in encouraging her female friends to examine their relationships. But what part she played, if any, in the Kautskys' troubled marriage is uncertain.

The argument did not run entirely in Luxemburg's favour, even on the left. Trotsky wrote to Kautsky that he could count on Lenin's support. 'I at any rate have not met a single comrade – not even among the Bolsheviks – who has come out openly for Luxemburg.'[157] Victor Adler, the Austrian socialist leader, told Bebel in the left's characteristically vituperative language, 'The poisonous bitch will yet do a lot of damage, all the more because she is as clever as a monkey, while on the other hand her sense of responsibility is totally lacking and her only motive is an almost perverse desire for self-justification.' Bebel – interestingly, remembering the accusation he had made against Luxemburg – replied, 'All that "Rosary" isn't as terrible as all that … with all the wretched female's squirts of poison, I wouldn't have the party without her.'[158] Kautsky himself even seemed to welcome the line that had now been drawn between him and Luxemburg, telling Adler that at least they would no longer been seen as the 'Siamese twins' of German socialism.

Luxemburg had challenged the SPD establishment at the party conference at Magdeburg in September 1910, which Kautsky was too fragile to attend. In a debate on universal suffrage she argued once more for mass strikes, but agreed to withdraw when it became obvious her motion had no prospect of success. Seeing the extent of her isolation, she wrote to Jogiches that evening, *I feel like a beaten dog, and it seems I've suffered a shattering defeat ... I am physically finished ... I cannot think, sleep or eat ... All my energy for the next two months to come has been used up by the party congress.*[159] Two weeks later she complained she was suffering such physical and moral depression she was unable to write a single word.

Luxemburg was shunned by the leadership as the party rallied for the 1912 Reichstag elections. She found it increasingly difficult to get the party press to accept her contributions. Only Clara Zetkin's *Die Gleichheit*, the socialist women's paper, and the *Leipziger Volkszeitung* were willing to print her article. In 1908 Luxemburg's friend Henriette Roland-Holst had threatened to resign from the Dutch socialists because of their lack of radicalism. Luxemburg advised against. *This you must not do, none of us must. We cannot stand outside the organisation, outside contact with the masses. The worst working class party is better than none.*[160] Luxemburg believed she had exposed Kautsky's Marxism as a sham and in the process her and Jogiches's project had foundered. But, beyond establishing another German party, there was nowhere else for the left to go. A loose radical alliance clung together in the party – Luxemburg, Franz Mehring, Clara Zetkin, and Karl Liebknecht prominent – united more by unhappiness with what they saw as the SPD's lack of socialist ambition than any realistic agenda. The main personalities met every Friday night in Berlin at the Rheingold restaurant, with Mehring presiding, grumbling at the sorry state of affairs.

Liebknecht had published a pamphlet in 1907 denouncing German militarism, earning himself 18 months' imprisonment for high treason. With Europe divided into two camps – the Triple Alliance of Germany, Austria and Italy, facing the Triple Entente of Britain, France and Russia – the left's focus shifted towards the danger of war, which it said flowed from imperialist rivalry. In May 1911 the British Foreign Secretary, Sir Edward Grey, proposed an international agreement to end what had become an arms race. The SPD welcomed the suggestion but Luxemburg derided it in the *Leipziger Volkszeitung*. If the European powers were serious, she said, they would give up their colonies and end their policy of carving out spheres of influence throughout the world. If they were not prepared to do that, rhetoric about limiting arms as a means of preventing conflict was fraudulent.

As if to confirm what Luxemburg was saying, Germany intervened again in Morocco in the summer of 1911, sending the warship *Panther* to Agadir. The Socialist International published a statement calling on all member parties to organise action against what appeared to be an imminent war. The SPD leaders disagreed: the German foreign ministry had assured them the government had no aggressive

Karl Liebknecht (1871–1919)

Son of Wilhelm Liebknecht, a founder of the SPD. After military service, Liebknecht became a lawyer in 1899. He joined the SPD in 1900 and was president of the Socialist Youth International from 1907–10. Liebknecht was elected to the Prussian parliament in 1908 and to the Reichstag in 1912. He voted for war credits in August 1914 but changed his position in December after helping establish the anti-war International Group (later the Spartacist League). Called up in 1915, he was imprisoned in 1916 for high treason. Released in October 1918, and a founder of the German Communist Party, Liebknecht was murdered in January 1919 following the abortive Spartacist Rising.

intentions. The party published an explanatory leaflet. Luxemburg released an internal SPD document, obtained through the Socialist International, showing the party leadership had been concerned more about the coming Reichstag elections than war and were afraid criticism of the government would provoke accusations that the SPD lacked patriotism. Luxemburg wrote in the *Leipziger*

Volkszeitung criticising what she saw as cowardice, support for colonialism and for Germany's imperial ambitions in particular. *In the whole of the leaflet there is not one word about the native inhabitants of the colonies, not a word about their rights, interests and sufferings because of the international policy. The leaflet repeatedly speaks of 'England's splendid colonial policy' without mentioning the periodic famine and spread of typhoid in India, extermination of the Australian aborigines and the hippopotamus-hide lash on the backs of the Egyptian fellah.*[161]

Already pushed to the margins, Luxemburg faced the full wrath of the party leadership at the SPD congress in Jena in September 1911. Bebel condemned what he said had been her 'serious indiscretion' in leaking a confidential document. When she put her case to the delegates, Bebel repeatedly interrupted from the chair. Luxemburg responded sarcastically, *When the party executive asserts something, I would never dare not to believe it, for as a faithful party member the old saying holds for me: Credo quia absurdum – I believe it precisely because it is absurd.*[162] The party executive, set on destroying what remaining influence Luxemburg had, took the issue to the International Socialist Bureau, seeking her censure and removal for a breach of discipline. The Bureau rejected the request. Luxemburg's relations with the SPD leadership were at breaking point but she remained defiant. *I won't let up on this gang and stand idly by*, she wrote to Clara Zetkin.[163]

∽

In August 1911 Luxemburg had moved from Friedenau to Lindenstrasse, a leafy street in the Berlin suburb of Südende. She later described the new flat – five rooms and a kitchen – in evocative language. *The clean, tidy room, full of sunshine, breathed such quiet and comfort. Through the open balcony door nothing intruded but the chirping of the sparrows, the hum of the electric tram which would pass*

Rosa Luxemburg in 1907.

once in a while, and the ringing metallic hammering of workers repairing rails somewhere. Then I would take my hat and go into the fields to look at what had grown during the night and collect fresh, succulent grass for Mimi. Mimi was Luxemburg's cat, whom she had found injured at the party school and nursed back to health. She made friends with a local shoemaker's children, who played in the street until dark. *And I would stand there, in the middle of the street, counting the first stars, not wanting to go home and get out of the mild air and the twilight in which the day and the night would softly nestle against one another.*[164] Luxemburg took her servant, Gertrude Zlottko, to the new flat with her.

Jogiches was barred from visiting the Lindenstrasse flat on any pretext, though Luxemburg – despite being well paid for her work at the party school – continued to ask him for money. Shortly after moving to Südende she begged a loan, saying it was urgent and she would be penniless if he failed to send it. A few months later she pleaded, *Can the party lend me 150–200 M by the first! I'll return it in a month together with the whole debt.*[165] The SDKPiL was itself in difficulties, not least because of Jogiches's authoritarianism. Luxemburg had lived with, and in the end rejected, his overbearing personality. She had vehemently criticised Lenin's similarly domineering attitude towards party organisation and, by extension, the working class. But Luxemburg was prepared to support Jogiches when he combined the two in the SDKPiL. In 1911 the activists in Warsaw split from the Berlin-based central committee. Julian Marchlewski, their old comrade and a joint founder of the party, said he could no longer tolerate Jogiches's arrogance. In May 1912 Jogiches, with Luxemburg's approval, declared the dissident Warsaw organisation disbanded, leaving an insignificant exile rump in Berlin. In the course of the SDKPiL rift, Luxemburg displayed a combination of intolerance towards disagreement and a personal spite, smearing her opponents and one individual in particular, Karl Radek.

Radek, long a political admirer of Luxemburg, had joined the SDKPiL in 1904 but opposed Jogiches in the argument leading to the split. Like Luxemburg, Radek was also an SPD member, active on the left in Bremen. Luxemburg and Jogiches now began a campaign of character assassination, insinuating through rumour that the Warsaw breakaway was riddled with police spies, a manoeuvre Luxemburg had suggested. They accused Radek – whom Luxemburg seemed particularly to dislike – of theft, embezzlement and being behind in his party subscription. When a party court could find no substance to the charges another court was convened and Radek resigned from the SDKPiL. Luxemburg and Jogiches then worked to ruin him politically by pressing the SPD to expel him. Luxemburg told Clara Zetkin, *Radek belongs to the whore category.*[166] Luxemburg wrote to Jogiches, *If we could prove Radek's guilt to the Germans beyond a reasonable doubt, it would be our salvation.*[167]

Luxemburg's political friends in Germany warned that her behaviour was excessive, but she continued to demand that the SPD executive – who were hardly her friends – should expel Radek. She relented at the last moment, at the party congress in 1913, when realisation dawned that achieving what she wanted might set a dangerous precedent for use against her and the left. Luxemburg's actions were revealing in their vindictiveness and inability to tolerate disagreement. This was Luxemburg in the exercise of power and the sight was not pleasant. Luxemburg and Radek would cross paths again dramatically in the final weeks of her life.

Relations were similarly fraught with the RSDLP. Luxemburg became involved in an attempt to manipulate re-unification of the Bolsheviks and Mensheviks through the SPD's control of money left to the Russian party by a wealthy sympathiser. The Bolsheviks, keen for finance but reluctant to co-operate, called an RSDLP congress in Prague in January 1912. Jogiches, a central committee member since 1907, refused to attend and the SDKPiL newspaper, *Red Banner*, described the congress as a 'farcical Leninist lark', implying sympathy for the Mensheviks. The Bolsheviks proceeded to establish a separate party, excluding the Mensheviks and the SDKPiL. The Mensheviks held their own congress in Vienna in August. Luxemburg and Jogiches, their Polish party in ruins and now having fallen out with both sides in the Russian argument, felt any influence they had had waning.

Finally, the SPD's success in the January 1912 elections seemed to vindicate Kautsky's 'strategy of attrition'. The party's vote rose from 3,259,000 to 4,250,000, a third of the electorate, and its seats from 43 to 110, making the SPD the largest group in the Reichstag, overtaking the Catholic Centre Party. Luxemburg had addressed rallies every evening for a month in the run-up to election day, avoiding controversy and urging her audience to vote for a party that in her heart she despised. When normal politics resumed, the arguments of Luxemburg and her few left-wing allies appeared irrelevant to most party members. She was seen, in the words of one historian, as 'an impractical dreamer and a likeable crank who was out of touch with day-to-day realities'.[168]

Sacrifice is part of the socialist's craft
1913–16

Bernstein had based his revisionism on his observation that capitalism, rather than being on the point of collapse, was thriving. The German Social Democrats had rejected the revisionist prognosis in theory, while following it in practice. This lay at the heart of Luxemburg's break with Kautsky and she persisted in her belief that capitalism faced inevitable doom. She had told the SPD's Hanover congress in 1899, when the campaign against Bernstein's revisionism was raging, that *the concept of a breakdown, of a social catastrophe ... a cataclysm* was what distinguished Marxism from reformism.[169] In her counterblast against Bernstein, *Social Reform or Revolution*, she wrote that scientific socialism was based on an understanding of *the growing anarchy of the capitalist economy, leading inevitably to its ruin*.[170] And yet, it survived.

The basic contradiction of capitalism can be briefly expressed. Capitalism as a system could produce ever more goods but to extract surplus value from their workers, to make a profit, employers had to pay them less than the value of what they made. The workers as a group therefore had insufficient money to buy what capitalism was producing, their total demand being unable to meet the total supply. Unsold goods would pile up, leading to slumps, depressions and mass unemployment as profits fell and employers reacted by cutting production. However, beyond temporary fluctuations, capitalism had so far evaded the cataclysmic final breakdown

Marxists considered inevitable. Why was this? An explanation had to be found for history's failure to move as forecast.

In preparing an *Introduction to Political Economy* for students at the party school, Luxemburg came up against what she saw as a crucial problem. It seemed to her that Marx had not fully explained in his major work *Das Kapital* whether capitalism could continue to develop indefinitely. In 1912 Luxemburg began writing *The Accumulation of Capital: A Contribution to an Explanation of Imperialism*, an attempt to explain capitalism's continuing survival and why this could only be short-term. Luxemburg later described to a friend her exalted creative state. *The period in which I wrote the Accumulation belongs to the happiest of my life. I lived in a veritable trance. Day and night I never saw nor heard anything as that one problem developed so beautifully before my eyes. I don't know which gave me more pleasure: the process of thinking, when I mulled over a complicated question slowly walking back and forth across the room, closely observed by Mimi, who lay on the red plush tablecloth, her little paws crossed, her intelligent head following me – or the literary creation with pen in hand. Do you know that I wrote the whole 900 pages in four months at one sitting. An unheard-of thing! Without checking the rough copy even once, I had it printed.*[171]

Luxemburg's conclusion was simple: imperialism was prolonging capitalism's life. Bernstein had given other explanations, revising Marxism in another way, only to be condemned by Luxemburg. The difference in Luxemburg's eyes was that she believed she was ironing out a tricky problem in the service of the revolution, while Bernstein was acting against it. In Luxemburg's revision, Marx was still correct but had been writing too soon to foresee imperialism. The major capitalist states were solving the problem of a lack of demand at home by colonising non-capitalist areas abroad, securing markets for their surplus production and seizing cheap supplies of raw materials and food. The logic of capitalism demanded aggression and exploitation for its own survival.

Between 1880 and 1910 the European powers had occupied 10 million square miles of Africa, with a population of 110 million, driven by capitalism's need for markets, but there were limits on the ability to expand into less developed areas. The resolution was temporary; collapse was inevitable once those markets had been exhausted. As a side issue, but one that was necessarily inter-linked, the armaments industry provided a further outlet, encouraging the international arms race. Capitalism, the competition for colonies and war were tied together.

The Accumulation of Capital, published in January 1913, was a complex work, intended for and only comprehensible to specialists who understood both Marxist and capitalist economics, as Luxemburg recognised. She wrote to an acquaintance, *From this standpoint {it was} a luxury and might just as well have been printed on the finest hand made paper.*[172] Her analysis was widely challenged, a particularly scathing review in the main SPD newspaper, *Vörwarts*, in February 1913 accusing her of solving a problem that did not exist. Sympathetic reviewers in regional party papers were vilified. Luxemburg said she could not recall another theoretical work by a Social Democrat having been treated so harshly (forgetting her onslaught on Bernstein in 1899). *All these events clearly indicate that there have been other passions touched on, one way or another, than 'pure science'.*[173]

Despite the 1912 revival, since 1907 the SPD had been influenced by the growing mood of nationalism and militarism in Germany. As tension between the European powers intensified, important sections of the party were finding their patriotic voice. Bebel, the party chairman and Luxemburg's early patron, died in 1913. Friedrich Ebert, a competent administrator who had risen through the trade union and SPD ranks, became co-chairman with Hugo

Haase. The party bureaucracy, bolstered by the increasingly right-wing trade unions and the burgeoning stratum of paid officials, had consolidated its position. Luxemburg's revolutionary political religion was out of step in a party intent on sturdy realism.

In March 1913 the SPD executive ordered all party newspapers to keep criticism of the leadership or Reichstag deputies out of their columns. Bernstein attempted to have Luxemburg removed from her post at the party school, but protests by her students saved her. In the summer a new editor was appointed to the *Leipziger Volkszeitung*. Luxemburg's contributions were first cut and then rejected. Mehring and Marchlewski resigned from the paper in solidarity. Having effectively censored the expression of left-wing views, the right triumphed at the party congress at Jena in September 1913. Two issues dominated the congress: the party's support for increased military spending and Luxemburg's perennial call for mass strikes. In June, 52 SPD Reichstag deputies had voted for property tax increases to meet a thousand million mark rise in the weapons bill, while 37 (the left, but also Bernstein) had voted against. Trotsky described Luxemburg's impact in the debates. 'Small in height and frail in build, she dominated the congress from the rostrum, like the incarnation of proletarian revolutionary thought. By the force of her logic and the power of her sarcasm she silenced her most sworn enemies.'[174]

Friedrich Ebert (1871–1925)

The son of a tailor, Ebert worked as a saddlemaker, entering politics and journalism through the trade union movement. An effective administrator who modernised the party bureaucracy, he became the SPD executive's secretary in 1905, was elected to the Reichstag in 1912 and appointed joint party chairman in 1913. He was at the forefront of the SPD's backing for war in 1914 but supported a munitions workers' strike in 1918. Appointed Reich Chancellor and then chairman of the Council of People's Commissars, he used the army and the Freikorps to suppress the left. Elected the Weimar Republic's first president in 1919, he held office until his death.

But Luxemburg's rhetoric – and her appeal for the congress, just for once, to accept a resolution from her – had no impact on a disciplined party. The congress backed increased military spending and rejected Luxemburg's appeal for mass strikes.

At the end of the year, Luxemburg, Mehring and Marchlewski – a small band on the left out of step with most party members – established a bulletin, *Socialdemocratische Korrespondenz*, to argue against what they feared was the triumph of revisionism. Mehring, knowing Luxemburg's tendency to fall out even with her friends, told a mutual acquaintance, 'Tell Rosa she mustn't upset me, as I'm her only supporter.'[175] The bulletin was run off on a duplicator at the office of a typist, Mathilde Jacob, who became a close companion of Luxemburg until her death. There was little chance of what Luxemburg and her comrades had to say appearing in the tightly-controlled party press and they were shouting into the wind. The criticisms of Kautsky and his policy of a step-by-step march through the Reichstag continued. The collapse of capitalism might be inevitable, Luxemburg said, but that did not mean waiting with arms folded until that happy day. *Leaders who hang back will certainly be pushed aside by the storming masses ... The task of Social Democracy and its leaders is not to be dragged along by events, but to be consciously ahead of them, to have an overall view of the trend of events, to shorten the period of development by conscious action,*

Mathilde Jacob (1873–1943)

Born in Berlin, the daughter of an assimilated Jewish meat trader. Living with her widowed mother and sister, Jacob ran a typing agency from home. She met Luxemburg in 1913 when she was engaged to type and duplicate *Socialdemocratische Korrespondenz*. Jacob became a close companion of Luxemburg and Jogiches, assisting in their anti-war organisation and maintaining the imprisoned Luxemburg's contact with life outside. After Luxemburg's death Jacob worked with Paul Levi in the German Communist Party but later rejoined the SPD. An anti-fascist, she maintained her typing business under the Nazis but was deported to a concentration camp, where she died.

and to accelerate its progress.[176] The rhetoric sounded stilted and over-heated, immaterial to a party intent on respectability.

Luxemburg now went on to do battle against the German state. In September 1913 she told an audience in Frankfurt am Main they must refuse to fire on fellow workers in the event of war. *If they expect us to lift the weapons of murder against our French or other foreign brothers, then let us tell them, 'No, we won't do it'.*[177] Luxemburg was arrested, charged with incitement to disobedience, and put on trial on 20 February 1914. Paul Levi, a 30-year-old socialist lawyer, acted for the defence. Luxemburg used her court appearance to make propaganda, delivering a remarkable speech later published as a pamphlet. War, she said, was the concern of the people, not only of the army. *Once the majority of working people come to the conclusion … that wars are nothing but a barbaric, unsocial, reactionary phenomenon, entirely against the interests of the people, then wars will have become impossible even if the soldiers obey their commanders.* One sentence would haunt her before the year was out. *We think that wars can only come about so long as the working class either supports them enthusiastically because it considers them justified and necessary, or at least accepts them passively.*[178]

Luxemburg was found guilty, sentenced to a year's imprisonment, but released pending her appeal. The prosecutor asked for a remand in custody lest she flee. Luxemburg interrupted, *Sir, I believe you would run away. A Social Democrat never does; he stands by his deeds and laughs at your punishments.*[179] And to a young Social Democrat she wrote, *My dear young friend, I assure you that I would not flee even were the gallows threatening, for the simple reason that I consider it thoroughly necessary to accustom our party to the fact that sacrifice is part of the socialist's craft and that this should be obvious.*[180] Invitations to speak and write flowed in as Luxemburg became a hero to party members once more.

∼

As if one sentence were not enough, Luxemburg challenged the authorities again in March 1914, charging them in an article in *Socialdemocratische Korrespondenz* and in a speech at Freiburg with physically and mentally abusing military conscripts. The Prussian Minister of War, General von Falkenhayn, accused her of insulting the army, a serious offence in a society dominated by supposed military virtues. Levi was engaged as a defence lawyer for what seemed an inevitable trial. Luxemburg and Levi had become lovers during the earlier case. Radical, sophisticated and highly educated, Levi represented – as one of Luxemburg's biographers suggested – her first 'adult relationship with an adult man'.[181] Jogiches had been incapable of the romantic love Luxemburg had craved and Costia Zetkin had been, emotionally at least, little more than a boy. After the affair with Zetkin had faltered, Luxemburg had a passionate friendship with Hans Diefenbach, a doctor who shared her tastes in music and literature. Writing to Diefenbach in 1917, Luxemburg recalled time they spent together in her Südende flat. *Nights when you would read Goethe aloud, between countless cups of tea, and I, with Mimi on the sofa, would give myself up to happy laziness …*[182]

Paul Levi (1883–1930)

Son of a Jewish banker, Levi became a radical lawyer and joined the SPD in 1906. Luxemburg's defence lawyer in 1914, he became her lover. Active in the anti-war movement after 1914, he briefly led the Spartacus League in 1918. Levi was a founder of the German Communist Party and became president of the United Communist Party in 1920. Expelled from the party following a failed Communist rising in 1921, he joined the Independent Social Democrats, finally returning to the SPD. In 1922 he edited and published Luxemburg's *The Russian Revolution*. Levi died after falling from a window.

In April Luxemburg and Levi took a holiday together at a cottage in Clarens, the village near Lake Geneva where she had previously stayed with Jogiches. Luxemburg began an intensive study of botany, systematically identifying and collecting flowers with the same rigour that she gave to the intricacies of Marxist theory. She later told a friend, *Now I am thoroughly at home in this green empire, which I conquered myself, by storm and with passion – and things you grasp with so much ardour strike firm roots in you.*[183] Luxemburg's relationship with Levi was as intensely political as that with Jogiches had been. After their return from Switzerland she wrote to Levi on 3 May, *Darling, that was so nice: on Monday you preached on imperialism in Frankfurt, on Tuesday I did in Charlottenburg.*[184] But this would be the last personal happiness Luxemburg experienced before her death. On 13 May Luxemburg told Levi she had received a notice of prosecution for her speech in March.

The trial was to begin on 29 June, but the authorities were already beginning to have second thoughts about the propaganda opportunity they were giving Luxemburg. Her accusations of military brutality had struck a chord not only with Social Democrats – the party newspaper *Vörwarts* was conducting its own campaign against corruption among senior officers – but in the wider population. Two weeks before Luxemburg was due to appear in court she had secured numerous witnesses prepared to testify to ill-treatment by the army. The trial was opened, adjourned and then adjourned again, this time for good. The day before Luxemburg's first appearance the heir to the Austro-Hungarian throne, Archduke Franz Ferdinand, and his wife had been assassinated in Sarajevo.

Austria accused Serbia of complicity in the Archduke's assassination. On 18 July, as the crisis developed, Luxemburg attended a meeting of the Socialist International in Brussels to discuss the continuing divisions among Russian Social Democrats. She pressed for the Bolsheviks to be expelled from the International unless they were prepared to re-unite with the Mensheviks. A week later, encouraged by Germany, Austria declared war on Serbia. The Russian government announced partial mobilisation of her army. The Socialist International hurriedly convened an emergency meeting in Brussels on 28 July, with most of the leading figures in European Social Democracy present, including Luxemburg and Kautsky, who were speaking again for the first time in four years. At its final session the following day the member parties of the Socialist International agreed to organise demonstrations pending resolution of the conflict between Austria and Serbia by arbitration. At a rally after the meeting Luxemburg sat silently, head in hands, refusing to address the crowd.

Europe stumbled into a war determined by pre-arranged plans for mobilisation and railway timetables. *Vörwarts*, the main SPD newspaper, was equivocal, calling Kaiser Wilhelm 'a sincere friend of the people's peace' but washing its hands of the looming danger. 'The Socialist proletariat refuses all responsibility for the events which are being conjured up by a ruling class blind to the point of madness.'[185] On 31 July the government declared martial law and imposed press censorship. The SPD were slowly moving into line, a speaker in the Reichstag saying that if war came, it would be against 'Russian despotism'. A regional party paper declared, 'We do not want our wives and children to be sacrificed to the bestialities of the Cossacks.'[186] But party members rallied to demonstrations against war, over 250 in 163 cities and towns involving three quarters of a million protestors, 30,000 at a Berlin meeting. On 31 July a French nationalist assassinated Jaurès, Luxemburg's old antagonist and friend, in Paris.

> **1914 timetable of war**
>
> Europe was enmeshed in a system of alliances, the Triple Alliance of Germany, Austria-Hungary and Italy facing the Triple Entente of Britain, France and Russia. On 28 June the heir to the Austro-Hungarian throne, Archduke Franz Ferdinand, was assassinated in Sarajevo. Austria-Hungary accused Serbia of involvement, declaring war on 28 July. Serbia's ally Russia mobilised on 31 July. Germany declared war on Russia on 1 August and on Russia's ally France on 3 August. Germany invaded Belgium to attack France and Britain declared war on Germany on 4 August. On 6 August Austria-Hungary declared war on Russia.

31 July 1914. Crowds hear the declaration of general mobilisation read by a lieutenant outside the Berlin Zeughas.

Germany declared war on Russia on 1 August, in an atmosphere less of popular enthusiasm than relief that the uncertainty had ended. The issue now facing the SPD was whether to vote the money necessary to pursue the conflict. The party leadership's room for manoeuvre narrowed on 1 August when the trade unions agreed they would not strike against the war in return for a promise from the government not to outlaw them. On 4 August, as German armies advanced into Belgium to attack France, and as Britain responded by declaring war on Germany, the SPD deputies supported the government's request for war credits of five million marks. In an earlier meeting 14 deputies had opposed this, including the party's leader in the Reichstag, Hugo Haase. But, accepting party discipline, Haase declared, contrary to his own feelings, 'In the hour of danger we will not desert our Fatherland.'[187] The SPD persuaded itself that the war was not an imperialist war but one of defence against Tsarist autocracy and barbarity. By September 1914 over a third of party members were in uniform, the majority reservists recalled to their regiments.

In a spirit of national unity the government permitted socialist literature in army barracks and allowed *Vörwarts* to continue publishing, provided there were no references to class struggle. On hearing that the party had not opposed the war, the Kaiser declared, 'I do not know parties anymore, I only know Germans.' The SPD press took on an increasingly xenophobic tone, formulating a socialist justification for war that went beyond self-defence against Russian barbarism and British imperialism. One writer subsequently argued that 'under the necessity of war socialist ideas have been driven into German economic life ... the national unity of state socialism.'[188] Luxemburg wrote in exasperation, *This party prostitutes itself in such a matter-of-fact way and with such good conscience as to deprive one of all illusions.*[189]

The outbreak of war, and the alacrity with which most of the SPD fell into line with the government, came as a shock to Luxemburg, personally and politically. She told her friend Luise Kautsky that she felt she was losing her mind and had contemplated suicide. Overnight her political identity had unravelled. The conflict represented to her the death of German socialism and the Socialist International. Her place in both as a rebel, the centre of her being, had become irrelevant. National sentiment, which she had persistently claimed was a delusion, had shown its hold on the working class, a class she had imagined differently. Nothing of what she and her comrades had been saying had had any impact. In her bitterness, she wrote that on 4 August 1914 *Social Democracy backed down without a struggle and conceded victory to imperialism.* The working class, she said, *broke like a reed in a storm.*[190] She recognised in a letter to a friend that she had been living an illusion before August 1914. *If things {in the SPD} were really like that and the whole peacetime glory was simply a will-o'-the-wisp on the swamp, then it is better that things come into the open.*[191] After all her denunciations of Kautsky and the party, Luxemburg was still capable of being surprised.

On the evening of the Reichstag vote, Luxemburg gathered a small group – Jogiches, Mehring, Marchlewski and a few others – at her Lindenstrasse flat. They agreed that Luxemburg should send telegrams to 300 regional party officials thought to be sympathetic, inviting them to a conference in Berlin. But only Luxemburg's friend Clara Zetkin, editor of the SPD women's paper *Die Gleichheit*, replied offering complete support. On 5 August, Karl Liebknecht – who had reluctantly voted for war credits – joined Luxemburg and her comrades in forming the International Group, declaring their opposition to the war. They were, as they half realised, beginning the process of establishing a new party. Luxemburg spoke at SPD meeting halls in the working class Neukölln district, giving the group's interpretation of the war's causes, hoping that – as she wrote to the Belgian socialist Camille Huysmans – *The working masses would take our side if it were possible to present our case.*[192] On 30 October the group placed a one-paragraph declaration in a Swiss newspaper dissociating themselves from the SPD's support for the war. Luxemburg wrote to Hans Diefenbach that she expected to be arrested any day. *I comfort myself that, at the end of the war, I will once again be able to breathe air.*[193] She shared the common belief that the conflict, however bloody, would at least be brief.

Luxemburg was now without an income. The SPD closed its school and, anyway, her views would hardly have been welcomed. Access to the party press was a thing of the past. Diefenbach said he could make 100 marks a month available to help with her living expenses. Luxemburg declined his offer. In December, weakened by anxiety and disappointment, she was taken into hospital in Schöneberg, exhausted. Liebknecht, meanwhile, had used his position as a deputy to observe what was happening in German-occupied Belgium. He returned to pose embarrassing questions in the Reichstag, asking how many Belgian civilians the army had shot in reprisals and for the government to release diplomatic papers on the reasons for the war. When the government sought further credits to finance the conflict on 2 December Liebknecht defied party discipline, casting a solitary vote against and denouncing what he called an imperialist war. In February 1915 he was called up for army service, the only SPD deputy to be conscripted, reputedly at the instigation of the party leadership.

Luxemburg left hospital, though still weak, and the International Group continued its activities underground, smuggling in foreign anti-war literature and producing a bulletin – *Die Internationale* – of which only one issue appeared. Luxemburg wrote the main article, 'Rebuilding the International'. She scorned attempts to justify the SPD's support for the war. *The global historical appeal of the Communist Manifesto undergoes a fundamental revision and, as amended by Kautsky, now reads: proletarians of all countries unite in peacetime and cut each other's throats in war!*[194] But before the bulletin appeared, Luxemburg was arrested on 18 February 1915. Police drove her first to their headquarters on Alexanderplatz and then to the Royal Prussian Prison for Women on Barnimstrasse to serve the sentence imposed a year earlier. She described her arrest to Mathilde Jacob in a letter from prison. *So that you didn't get any exaggerated ideas about my heroism, I'll confess, repentantly, that when I had to strip to my chemise and submit to a frisking for the second time that day, I could barely hold back the tears. Of course, deep inside, I was furious with myself at such weakness, and I still am.*[195]

The SPD paid a 60-mark fee to the authorities to exempt Luxemburg from prison work, allowing her the leisure to read and write. Diefenbach kept up the rent on her flat, while Jacob took care of Mimi the cat, *The highest honour I can award a mortal being*, Luxemburg wrote.[196] Luxemburg was allowed two days of liberty in early March to arrange her affairs and spent the time at her flat talking to Mehring, Levi, Jogiches and Liebknecht. Returned to custody, she wrote to Marta Rosenbaum (a longstanding party comrade) on 12 March, *On the whole I am in a very good and confident mood. History is really working into our hands.*[197]

Luxemburg quickly established a routine to get her through her sentence. Up at 5.40 a.m. and in bed at 9 p.m., reading and writing during the day and early evening, identifying flowers in a small patch of garden and studying the birds that landed in a courtyard. *My prison cell was as clean as a jewel box*, she told Mathilde Jacob.[198] She wrote letters to Jacob (22 in all), Clara Zetkin, Marta Rosenbaum and Luise Kautsky. But most of her writing was devoted to *Anti-Critique*, a response to criticisms of the *Accumulation of Capital*, and to a long pamphlet on what the war had exposed as a crisis of social democracy. Luxemburg's friends evaded the visiting rules on a variety of pretexts: Jacob as her secretary, Zetkin as her sister-in-law and Liebknecht – allowed leave from his regiment when the Reichstag was sitting – as her lawyer. Each of them smuggled papers hidden in newspapers and books to keep her in touch with developments in the International Group and carried drafts of articles and leaflets out. Security, given wartime conditions and Luxemburg's radical reputation, was remarkably lax. Liebknecht, prompted by his wife, ensured Luxemburg was supplied with what she mockingly called *life's little ornaments*, soap, combs and nightdresses.

In April 1915 Luxemburg (writing under the pen-name 'Junius') completed the draft of *The Crisis of Social Democracy*, dissecting every illusion of the pre-war SPD and the Socialist International, which in truth she had shared. There had been no swift victory in the war, she said, no cathartic if temporary resolution of capitalism's crisis. *The show is over. The curtain has fallen on trains filled with reservists, as they pull out amid the joyous cries of enthusiastic maidens. We no longer see their laughing faces, smiling cheerily from the train windows upon a war-mad population. Quietly they trot through the streets, with their sacks upon their shoulders. And the public, with a fretful face, goes about its daily task.*[199]

She asked whether war had been inevitable, whether the Socialist International could have held back the rush. *The great historical hour of the world war obviously demanded a unanimous political accomplishment, a broad-minded, comprehensive attitude that only the Social Democracy is destined to give. Instead ... Social Democracy did not adopt the wrong policy – it had no policy whatsoever.* Only revolution could end the war and prevent such an abomination occurring again, Luxemburg said. *Another such war, and the hope of socialism will be buried under the ruins of imperialistic barbarism ... Here capitalism reveals its death's head, here it betrays that it has sacrificed its historic right of existence, that its rule is no longer compatible with the progress of humanity.* The war offered a lesson. *If the proletariat learns from this war and in this war to exert itself, to cast off its serfdom to the ruling classes, to become the lord of its own destiny, the shame and misery will not have been in vain.*[200]

Germany's military strategy had been based on crushing France in six weeks before turning to face what was seen as the more formidable Russian army. In the event, there had been successes against Russia but, following a lightning German advance through Belgium, by 1915 the Western Front had stagnated into lines of trenches across northern France. The population and the SPD were now feeling the pressures of war. In June 1915 a thousand party officials presented the SPD executive with a petition calling for a negotiated peace. An anti-war rump of the Socialist International met in Zimmerwald, Switzerland, in September 1915, divided on whether the war was a revolutionary opportunity, as Lenin argued, or a horror to be ended at any cost. Luxemburg's contribution, a paper proposing a new International with sufficient authority to prevent the national fragmentation of 1914, arrived too late for debate. The conference represented the beginning of the end of the coalition between revolutionary and reformist socialism, as had the rise of the International Group in Germany. In October women in Berlin, many now working in the arms industries, demonstrated against rising prices and protestors fought the police. The SPD dismissed Clara Zetkin as editor of *Die Gleichheit* in 1915, signalling that they had disowned her. She was arrested soon after. On 21 December the government sought a further 10 billion marks in war credits. Twenty SPD deputies voted against in the Reichstag and a further 22 abstained.

On 1 January 1916 – with Luxemburg still in prison – anti-war Socialists held a secret and illegal conference in Berlin, establishing the Spartacus League, named in honour of the gladiator who had led a slave revolt against the Roman Empire. Luxemburg wrote the League's guiding principles in her prison cell, accusing the SPD leadership of treason and calling for the resumption of the class struggle. *The fatherland of all proletarians is the Socialist International, and defence of this must take priority over everything else.*[201] On 27 January, the Kaiser's birthday, the Spartacists issued the first of a series of letters, abusing the Kaiser and the SPD equally.

The Reichstag party caucus expelled Liebknecht as Luxemburg was being released on 18 February. The authorities either did not realise the extent of her involvement with the Spartacists or regarded the new group as insignificant. The police hustled a demonstration of Socialist women at the prison gate into a nearby park, but a few remained, with Liebknecht carrying bunches of flowers. Luxemburg protested, *I could not have dreamt that such nonsense would be organised. The women would be better occupied mending their husbands' socks and doing the housekeeping.* At her flat in Südende, Luxemburg took Mimi the cat in her arms, while her friends welcomed her with gifts of food, already in short supply. Exhausted, unused to company and weakened by the year in Barnimstrasse, Luxemburg went to bed early, asking Jacob, *Oh, why is everything all right just for me?*[202]

I feel so little inclination for the impending brawl 1916–18

Sick and frequently in pain, Luxemburg was to enjoy only five months of freedom. She addressed groups of sympathisers at clandestine meetings across Germany, always in danger of arrest, and wrote leaflets for distribution in factories and to be smuggled to soldiers at the Front. Liebknecht and his wife Sonia were frequent visitors to Luxemburg's home. In March 1916 Luxemburg, Liebknecht and Jogiches held a conference of radical oppositionists, planning anti-war street demonstrations for 1 May, May Day, the international workers' celebration. Handbills called workers in Berlin to a rally in the Potsdamer Platz at 8 p.m.

As the hour approached, thousands had gathered, surrounded by police. Liebknecht, Luxemburg at his side, shouted to the crowd, 'Down with the war. Down with the government'. The police seized him before he could go on and took him to the station, Luxemburg following behind. She returned to the demonstration to see mounted police riding into the crowd, striking out with batons. The protestors fought back, singing revolutionary anthems as the cavalry dispersed them into side streets. Liebknecht was accused of 'aiding a hostile power' and sentenced to 30 months imprisonment in July. Luxemburg wrote in a leaflet calling for a strike on the day he was sentenced, *The police truncheons can drive you from the streets, but no power on earth can force you into the workshops*.[203] Liebknecht appealed against his sentence but in

August the court increased the term to four years. Over 50,000 workers in Berlin went on strike for the day.

Liebknecht was hailed throughout Europe as the standard-bearer of the anti-war left. The SPD leaders, tied to the state in their backing for the war, tried to minimise the impact of his gesture, saying a barking dog did not bite. Luxemburg turned on her old comrades. *A dog is someone who, at his government's command, abjures, slobbers, and tramples down into the muck the whole history of his party and everything it has held sacred for a generation.*[204] Ernest Meyer took over the day-to-day leadership of the Spartacus League on Liebknecht's arrest, until he himself was seized in August. Responsibility passed to Jogiches, who moved from the hotel in Steglitz, where he lived under an assumed name, to lodge with a soldier's widow.

On 7 July 1916 Luxemburg sent Liebknecht's wife Sonia a postcard from Leipzig, where she had gone to address a meeting. She said she had sat in a park for two hours reading Galsworthy. *My contacts with people are ever less satisfying. I believe that soon I really will withdraw to anchorism like St Anthony, but – without 'temptations'.*[205] She returned to Berlin on 9 July to prepare for a holiday in Thuringia with Mathilde Jacob. The following day two detectives arrested Luxemburg at her flat. They allowed her a hurried breakfast while Jacob packed a suitcase. She was taken first to Potsdamer Platz by train and then by taxi to Barnimstrasse Prison, where the authorities told her she was being held in 'preventive custody' as a threat to state security. Mehring and Marchlewski, both Spartacus members, were arrested at the same time, allegedly at the request of SPD leaders embarrassed by growing divisions over the war.

Mimi, the cat to which Luxemburg was so attached, the baby she had never had, remained in the flat at Lindenstrasse in Jacob's care. The cat could have accompanied Luxemburg once definite arrangements had been made for her imprisonment but she explained to Sonia Liebknecht, *The little creature is used to cheer-fulness and life. She likes it when I sing, laugh, or chase her through all the rooms. Surely, she would become melancholy here.*[206] Mimi was ill in 1917, though Luxemburg's friends kept the news secret for months. When Luxemburg discovered the truth she told Jacob she felt she could no longer trust her. But Mimi's death later in the year was also kept from her.

Conditions in Barnimstrasse were relatively liberal for uncon-victed prisoners, which Luxemburg was, the authorities allowing books and gifts. Jacob's mother prepared meals suitable for Lux-emburg's delicate stomach. These were delivered every day and Luxemburg was able to hide notes in the empty dishes before they left the prison. But in September 1916, angered by a guard's interruption during a visit from Jacob, Luxemburg threw a bar of chocolate and called him a 'filthy spy'. She was transferred that evening to a cell in the Berlin police headquarters at Alexander-platz, badly lit and almost unbearably noisy with the constant clatter of passing trains and trams. Luxemburg wrote to a friend, *The month and a half I spent there turned my hair grey and left me with nerves wrecked so badly that I'll never be the same.*[207]

At the end of October 1916 Luxemburg was moved again, this time to the prison fortress of Wronke in Prussian Poland, a red-brick building, grim and overpowering, set – as if to taunt the prisoners – in idyllic countryside. Luxemburg was allocated a house inside the walls, with a living room, bedroom and small private garden. On 31 October she asked Jacob to send money – she had to pay four marks a week for privileges, books, clothes and soap. Jacob visited in November, staying a week in the nearby town. Luxemburg told Jacob she felt comfortable in her accom-modation and that the prison authorities were friendly, allowing special meals to be brought in. But her sentence was indetermi-nate, with no release date on the horizon. Jacob found her friend's sense of helplessness increasing, particularly when a new and less amenable supervisor took charge. Jacob wrote of one visit in her memoir of Luxemburg, 'Rosa sat on my lap, leaned her head on my shoulder and allowed tendernesses which she normally did not tolerate.'[208]

Luxemburg set herself a routine, making an effort to feel she had an element of control over her life inside. She read, wrote – translating into German the autobiography of the Russian writer and revolutionary Vladimir Korolenko – observed and identified the birds around the prison and tended her garden. She described to Diefenbach a morning in May watering flowers. *The water spray twinkled in the morning sun and the drops go shimmering for a long time on the blue and red hyacinths, which are already half open. Why am I sad in spite of this?*[209] Luxemburg also struggled to preserve the self that had existed in the world outside prison. She wrote articles for the Spartacus League, smuggled out by Jacob to Jogiches, and letters to her friends, reminiscing about the past, describing her present feelings and hopes for the future. *I feel at home anywhere in the world where there are clouds and birds and human tears*, she wrote to Mathilde Wurm in February 1917.[210]

∾

The German high command's hope in 1914 for a short war was based on political as well as military calculations. They had little confidence in Austria-Hungary as an ally and knew that in a protracted conflict the combination of Britain, France and Russia outweighed Germany militarily and industrially. Domestically, they feared the pressure war would impose on the population. Helmuth von Moltke the Younger, the Chief of the General Staff, had warned the Kaiser in 1906 that he foresaw 'a war which will utterly exhaust our own people, even if we are victorious'.[211] By 1916 the German population were in a desperate condition. As early as 1915 bread was being made from potatoes and substitutes were increasingly

(From left to right) Field Marshal von Hindenburg, Kaiser Wilhelm II and General Ludendorff during the First World War.

necessary for food and raw materials as the British tightened the blockade on imports. In the winter of 1916–17 the potato harvest failed and turnips became the main source of food. The calorific value of workers' rations was half an adult's requirement. As the army demanded more men for the front, industrial conscription was imposed to keep the factories operating. There were as many women as men working in industry.

In August 1916 Germany became a military dictatorship in all but name under the new Chief of the General Staff Field Marshal Paul von Hindenburg and his deputy General Erich Ludendorff. As popular discontent mounted, events were moving in the direction the Spartacus League – kept alive as an organisation by Jogiches and injected with enthusiasm by Luxemburg's articles – hoped and had expected. Divisions were growing in the SPD over the war. Luxemburg advised against an outright split, writing in an article smuggled from Wronke by Jacob in January 1917 that this would leave the party in the hands of its enemies. But in April the SPD expelled Reichstag deputies who had voted against further war credits, leading to the creation of a separate

Independent Social Democratic Party of Germany (USPD). The USPD gathered a diverse group of the pre-1914 SPD's theoreticians, including Kautsky of the 'Marxist centre' and Bernstein, the apostle of revisionism, only their hopes of a negotiated peace holding them together. The Spartacus League attached itself to the USPD, as out of place as it had been with the SPD. Radicals in Bremen, Hamburg and Dresden refused to follow the Spartacus League into the USPD, arguing that the time had come for a complete break with Social Democracy. In April munitions workers struck in protest against a reduction in the bread ration, 300,000 in Berlin and thousands more throughout Germany. In July the 'Reichstag majority' – the SPD, the Catholic Centre Party and the left liberals – pressed for a peace without annexations or reparations, together with constitutional reform.

~

Luxemburg's letters from prison reflected her changing moods, from depression to elation, as she acted before her limited audience. Hans Diefenbach, a pre-war friend and now a doctor in the army, was transformed in her mind into a lover. She joked that the war was going badly because of his affairs with French women, but also revealed her despair. In one letter she described days they had spent together, her memories of happiness. *I fear that after the war*

Independent Social Democrats (USPD)

A minority of the SPD – including 18 Reichstag deputies – that broke away in April 1917 in opposition to continuing the war. The USPD's main figures were the leading theoreticians Karl Kautsky, Eduard Bernstein and Hugo Haase. They called for a negotiated peace, with 'neither victors nor vanquished'. Luxemburg's Spartacist League attached itself to the USPD. The USPD briefly shared power with the SPD in the post-November revolution Council of People's Commissars. By 1920 the USPD had 750,000 members but split, the majority allying with the Communists to establish the United Communist Party. In 1922 the USPD merged with the SPD.

quiet and comfort will cease to exist entirely. And by God I feel so little inclination for the impending brawl.[212] In a similar spirit she wrote to Luise Kautsky, *I must have someone who will believe that I am whirling in the maelstrom of world history only by mistake and was in fact born to tend geese.*[213] Troubled by persistent stomach pain and migraine, often hardly able to eat, she wrote to Jacob, *I am suffering from mental depression. At times it is so bad that I have serious fears.*[214]

Luxemburg could also be harsh to friends too weak to share her self-sacrifice. In a letter to Mathilde Wurm in December 1916 she condemned the so-called radicals who failed to follow her. *You aren't radical at all, just spineless ... you are a totally different zoological species from me and never have I hated your miserable, acidulated, cowardly and half-hearted existence as much as I do now ... The world is so beautiful in spite of all the misery and would be even more beautiful if there were no half-wits and cowards in it.*[215] In February 1917 she told Wurm, *My dear girl, 'disappointment with the masses' is always the most lamentable excuse for a political leader. A real leader doesn't adjust his tactic in accordance with the attitude of the masses, but in accordance with the development of history. He sticks to his tactic in spite of disappointment and waits for history to complete its work.*[216] Frustrated, ill and lonely, Luxemburg let her Marxist self-confidence slip into arrogance, using 'History' as a comforting prop.

But history returned to save Luxemburg: revolution in Russia. In April 1917 she wrote to Marta Rosenbaum, *The wonderful events in Russia affect me like a life-giving elixir. It must, it will have a redeeming effect in the whole world.*[217] After weeks of violent demonstrations by civilians, and a refusal by the army to fire on them, Tsar Nicholas II abdicated on 15 March, persuaded by his generals that this might save Russia from defeat by Germany. The Duma formed a provisional government under Prince Lvov, while workers and soldiers in Petrograd established a Soviet, jostling for power. The new administration was determined to continue the war, the Soviet to end it. Grasping scraps of news from out-of-date newspapers, Luxemburg wrote a hurried article for the *Spartacus Letter* calling for a democratic republic in Russia and peace. The *Spartacus Letter* was a radical anti-war bulletin produced by Luxemburg's comrades, which circulated illegally in Germany and reached soldiers in the trenches.

In May she urged European workers to follow their Russian comrades and rise against their rulers. But the pain of imprisonment remained. She told Sonia Liebknecht at the end of May, *To be sure, it is rare enough that I get the temptation to speak. I don't even hear my own voice for weeks on end.*[218] A week later she wrote, *Inwardly I feel much more at home in a plot of garden like the one here, and still more in the meadows when the grass is humming with bees, than at one of our party congresses. Surely I can tell you this, since you will not immediately suspect me of betraying socialism! You know I hope to die at my post, in a street fight or in jail. But the real deep 'me' belongs more to my butterflies than it does to my comrades.*[219]

In July the USPD and the International Socialist Bureau tried unsuccessfully to secure Luxemburg's release on health grounds, hoping to have her moved to Russia. Instead, on 22 July, she was transferred to another prison, this time in Breslau. More strictly confined in harsher conditions, Luxemburg gave way to hopelessness, telling Jacob, *I shall perish here.* The authorities allowed her a second room and Jacob found a socialist family nearby willing to cook and deliver meals. The prison doctor shared Luxemburg's affection for Goethe and secured her a ticket for the nearby university library. But Luxemburg's sense of isolation intensified and her influence on the Spartacus League waned as she contributed less and less to its publications. In October Luxemburg resisted a further attempt at repatriation to Russia. *No, I remain at my post, and I still hope to experience something in Germany, and in the not too distant future at that.*[220]

In November Luxemburg received the news that Diefenbach had been killed in France. He left Luxemburg 50,000 marks, to be held in trust, with 4 per cent interest paid annually. 'I make this disposition,' Diefenbach said in his will, 'because my excellent friend may not prove as great a genius in her personal economy as in her understanding of the economics of a whole society.'[221] Luxemburg complained the interest was hardly enough to cover half her rent and expenses. But Diefenbach's death struck her deeply, as she told Sonia Liebknecht. *I firmly believe that, in the end, after the war, or at the close of the war, everything will turn out all right. But apparently we must first wade through a period of the worst human suffering.*[222]

In April 1917 Lenin had travelled from Switzerland through Germany to Sweden and onto Russia in transport provided by the German government. Luxemburg's former friend Alexander Parvus-Helphand, now an agent for the German foreign ministry, negotiated arrangements with the government, which also – it was alleged but never proven – gave Lenin money to strengthen his party. The Bolsheviks in power would, Germany hoped, overturn the provisional regime and remove Russia from the war. On his arrival in Petrograd Lenin criticised party members for limiting their ambitions to establishing a parliamentary republic and said they should be looking to socialism. He urged peasants to seize the land and workers the factories. But while peace and expropriation of industry were compatible with socialism, extending individual ownership of land contradicted the Marxist project. In July Bolsheviks were involved in a half-hearted coup against the provisional government. Alexander Kerensky, Prince Lvov's successor, retaliated by accusing Lenin of being a German agent and ordered his arrest. Lenin fled to Finland but returned to Petrograd when Kerensky was reduced to seeking Bolshevik help against a rebel general.

On 7 November Bolshevik Red Guards occupied strategic buildings in Petrograd and attacked the Winter Palace, headquarters of the Provisional Government, arresting ministers in a virtually bloodless coup. The revolution hardly resembled the overthrow of a mature capitalist society Marxists had envisaged, more the kind of utopian putsch Marx and Engels had condemned. The Bolsheviks had some working class support in Petrograd, but industrial workers made up only 2 per cent of Russia's overwhelmingly peasant population. Russia was undergoing a peasant revolution led by a party claiming to represent the working class. The All-Russia Congress of Soviets passed state authority to the Council of People's Commissars, made up entirely of Bolsheviks, pending election of a constituent assembly. In voting at the end of the month, the Social Revolutionaries (strong among the peasantry) won 299 seats, the Bolsheviks 168, the Mensheviks 18 and the liberal Constitutional Democrats 17. The assembly met on 5 January 1918, rejected the Bolshevik programme, and was dissolved by Lenin. 'Without the revolution in Germany, we are doomed,' Lenin was reported to have said.[223] By 'we' he meant the Bolsheviks.

Luxemburg knew little of the details of the Bolshevik coup. She wrote to Luise Kautsky, *Are you happy about the Russians? Of course, they will not be able to maintain themselves in this witches' Sabbath … because Social Democracy in the highly developed West consists of miserable and wretched cowards who will look quietly on and let the Russians bleed to death.*[224] At the end of January 1918 a Revolutionary Shop Stewards committee in Berlin led a general strike of half a million munitions workers demanding 'Peace, freedom, bread', a slogan that had echoed through Petrograd. Friedrich Ebert, now leader of the SPD in the Reichstag, showed some sympathy to the strikers and was appointed chairman of the strike committee. Ebert used his position to attempt to mediate an end to the strike, earning the enmity of the left as a traitor to the working class and the right as a traitor to the nation. The action abated as the government pressed strikers into the army. Jogiches, ignoring Luxemburg's plea that he should flee to Switzerland, was arrested in March. Paul Levi – Luxemburg's pre-war lawyer and lover – took over production and distribution of the Spartacus Letters.

Through the summer of 1918 Luxemburg wrote her impressions of the Russian revolution. What she had to say was supportive, but also perceptively critical given the difficulties in obtaining reliable information. Levi, reading a draft and sharing the reluctance of his fellow Spartacists to undermine the Bolsheviks, appealed to Luxemburg not to reveal her doubts publicly. But in September she told him, *I am writing this pamphlet only for you and if I can convince you then the effort isn't wasted.*[225] Her analysis of the Russian Revolution remained unpublished until 1922.

Luxemburg's ambivalence shone through. While she praised the Bolsheviks for their decisiveness, it is difficult to find one of their actions that she did not criticise. She surely knew that the Petrograd coup was the work of a minority of a minority, not the spontaneous mass rising of the working class she had always imagined. But she condemned 'opportunists' – Kautsky and the Mensheviks – who claimed Russia was only ready for a bourgeois rather than a proletarian revolution (though in April she herself had called only for a democratic republic in Russia). She praised Lenin and Trotsky for bringing honour to the socialist movement. But, she added tellingly, *Surely nothing can be further from their thoughts than to believe that all the things they have done or left undone … should be regarded by the International as a shining example of socialist policy towards which only critical admiration and zealous imitation are in order.*[226] She pointed to the dangers in Lenin's reliance on the peasants, the millions he had encouraged to seize land for themselves. They would stubbornly resist any attempt to socialize their newly-gained private property.

Above all, Luxemburg criticised the Bolsheviks for dismissing the constituent assembly. She agreed every democratic institution had shortcomings, but said the remedy Lenin and Trotsky had chosen was worse than the disease they were seeking to cure. If they were not satisfied that the assembly reflected the new conditions, they should have called fresh elections. *Freedom only for the supporters of the government, only for members of one party – however numerous they may be – is no freedom at all. Freedom is always and exclusively freedom for the one who thinks differently. Not because of any fanatical concept of 'justice' but because all that is instructive, wholesome and purifying in political freedom depends on this essential characteristic, and its effectiveness vanishes when 'freedom' becomes a special privilege.* The argument of 1904 with Lenin had returned, in reality rather than theory. She disagreed with what she described as his assumption *that the socialist transformation is something for which a ready-made formula lies completed in the pocket of the revolutionary party, which needs only to be carried out energetically in practice.*[227] But what were the Bolsheviks to do: risk being a minority in a fresh assembly? Luxemburg said nothing about the soviets, which the Bolsheviks would first dominate and then suck the life from.

Luxemburg may have been confused, but she could still be bleakly prophetic. *Without general elections, without unrestricted freedom of press and assembly, without a free struggle of opinion, life dies out in every public institution, becomes a mere semblance of life, in which only the bureaucracy remains active. Public life gradually falls asleep, a few dozen party leaders of inexhaustible energy and boundless experience direct and rule. Among them, in reality only a dozen outstanding heads do the leading and an elite of the working class is invited from time to time to meetings where they applaud the speeches of the leaders, and approve proposed resolutions unanimously …*[228] And yet, the Bolsheviks had taken power and, for all her doubts, Luxemburg's heart was with them. They had, she said, posed a question that only the European working class, and most of all the German workers, could answer. Luxemburg wrote to a friend, *Enthusiasm coupled with the spirit of revolutionary criticism – what more can people want from us?*[229]

A beginning has been made 1918–19

Germany's war with Russia ended in March 1918 with the Treaty of Brest-Litovsk. The army launched an offensive on the Western Front in the spring, hoping to secure a success before significant numbers of American troops arrived in France. But by late summer Germany was on the point of collapse as the Allies regained lost ground and advanced towards Belgium. War-weary soldiers deserted in their thousands, roaming behind the lines and in Germany. Isolated in Breslau prison in the third year of her confinement, Luxemburg knew little of this. In June she described her anger with a working class still loyal to the Kaiser. *The German worker is tramping, wading over knee-deep in blood, onward, to plant the victorious banner of German imperialism everywhere.*[230] On 29 September Field Marshal von Hindenburg and General Ludendorff admitted to the Kaiser that defeat was inevitable. They urged him to seek an armistice and at least give the appearance of democratising the government to secure favourable terms and save the monarchy.

On 3 October the Kaiser called on his cousin, Prince Max of Baden, to replace Count Georg von Hertling as Imperial Chancellor. Prince Max appointed a cabinet of representatives of the Catholic Centre Party, the Democratic Party and the SPD. The SPD's Philipp Scheidemann and Otto Barth were well aware that the new government's role was to take responsibility for the regime's defeat but feared that without an orderly transfer of power the collapse might lead to a Bolshevik-style revolution. The German population, dispirited, weak from hunger, already succumbing to the virulent Spanish influenza epidemic sweeping Europe, were told the government was seeking an armistice on 5 October. The Spartacists, as bemused as anyone by the sudden revelation of the German Empire's impotence, called for a rising to create 'conditions of freedom for the class struggle of the workers, for a real democracy, for a real and lasting peace and for Socialism'.[231]

On 12 October the government declared an amnesty for political prisoners, but Luxemburg remained in custody, ineligible for release as she had never been convicted. She wrote to a friend on 18 October that in the midst of the events sweeping Germany imprisonment was unbearable. *When the general swing in the situation occurred, something psychological in me also snapped. The conversations under surveillance, with no possibility of talking about the things that really interest me, have now become such a burden that I would prefer to do without any visits at all, until we can see each other as free people ... Anyway, it can't last much longer.*[232] Liebknecht was freed on 23 October, greeted by crowds in Berlin and driven direct to the Russian Embassy for a celebratory dinner. He took over leadership of the Spartacist League and was co-opted into the Revolutionary Shop Stewards, a group formed from factory workers in the January 1918 strikes.

Germany was now a constitutional monarchy and for the SPD leader, Friedrich Ebert, the party's long-sought objective had been gained, without the civil violence he had feared. The 'revolution from above' was over. But on 28 October German naval commanders ordered the fleet into the North Sea for a final battle with the British, against the wishes of a government negotiating an armistice with the Allies. The crews on two ships refused to continue when the ships were at sea. The mutiny was suppressed and the rebels were transported to Kiel for court martial. But on 3 November sailors and shipyard workers in Kiel demonstrated for their release, and the following day a sailors' council took over the town, sending deputations to ports along the coast to spread the revolt.

The SPD despatched Gustav Noske, its military specialist, to Kiel to prevent what the government regarded as a mutiny becoming more dangerous. Noske persuaded the council to appoint him as chairman and calmed matters. But the revolt had spread, with councils of workers, sailors and soldiers now controlling Wilhelmshaven, Cuxhaven and Hamburg, the first major city to come under council authority. Over the next few days Brunswick, Hanover, Munich fell as workers and soldiers spontaneously established councils. In Bavaria the king fled and Kurt Eisner, the local Independent Socialist (USPD) leader, emerged at the head of a socialist republican government.

The new government in Berlin now feared a different revolution was gaining strength, aware that the left of the USPD and the Revolutionary Shop Stewards were planning a rising in the capital. On 6 November Ebert and the SPD executive met Prince Max and General Wilhelm Groener, who had replaced Ludendorff as army Chief of Staff. Ebert warned that only the Kaiser's abdication would save the monarchy. The following day Prince Max asked Ebert what position the SPD would take if the Kaiser did renounce the throne. Could he as Chancellor count on the party's support against revolution in the streets? Prince Max noted Ebert's reply in his diary. 'If the Kaiser does not abdicate,

Wilhelm Groener (1867–1939)

Groener joined the army in 1884 and by 1914 had responsibility for the movement of troops by rail. In 1916 he was appointed head of food supply and then of war production, becoming close to Hindenburg and Ludendorff, the country's military dictators, and forming relationships with SPD and trade union leaders. Groener was instrumental in persuading the Kaiser to abdicate and in gaining the army command's support for Ebert. Transport Minister from 1920–3, Groener became Defence Minister in 1928 and Interior Minister in 1931. He was forced to resign in 1932 after attempting to ban the Nazi Brownshirts.

the social revolution is inevitable. I do not want it – in fact, I hate it like sin.'[233]

～

The prison authorities in Breslau told Luxemburg she was to be released at 10 p.m. on 8 November. With such scant warning, she spent one more night in custody, going next morning to the railway union offices in the town. Finding that civilian trains were running only as far as Frankfurt-an-der-Oder, Luxemburg joined a revolutionary demonstration in Breslau, addressing the crowds from the city hall balcony. When she telephoned Mathilde Jacob in Berlin Jogiches, released on 8 November and still weak from flu, suggested Jacob went by car to Frankfurt to meet Luxemburg. The car broke down. Luxemburg, travelling overnight on a packed military train, sitting on her suitcase, arrived at Schlesischer station in Berlin on 10 November. Her biographer Frölich, who saw her soon after her arrival, described the distressing impact of Luxemburg's appearance on her friends. 'She had aged terribly, and her black hair had gone quite white. She was a sick woman.'[234] Luxemburg, confused by the crowds of soldiers and workers filling the streets, telephoned Jacob from the station, to be told by Jacob's mother that her daughter was on her way to Frankfurt. Luxemburg went to Jacob's flat, where Liebknecht and Levi greeted her.

The Spartacists had seized the offices and printing press of the conservative *Berliner Lokal-Anzeiger* the previous day but were only able to run off an evening and morning edition of the party's new paper, *Die Rote Fahne* (*The Red Flag*), before the workers had second thoughts about involving themselves in radical propaganda. Levi and Liebknecht took Luxemburg directly from Jacob's flat to the paper's offices, giving her no time to rest. She was unable to persuade the printers to change their minds. Luxemburg, Jogiches, Liebknecht and Levi took rooms at the Hotel Excelsior, setting up a ramshackle Spartacus headquarters. Later that evening Jacob collected Luxemburg's luggage from the station. Jacob later wrote, 'When I returned to Rosa Luxemburg's room, Karl Liebknecht was standing with her at the window and admiring the starry sky.'[235] Luxemburg had written a few months before what she said was as the basic lesson of every revolution. *Either the revolution must advance at a rapid, stormy, and resolute tempo, break down all barriers with an iron hand and place its goals even farther ahead, or it is quite soon thrown backward behind its feeble point of departure and suppressed by counter-revolution. To stand still, to make time on one spot, to be contended with the first goal it happens to reach, is never possible in revolution.*[236]

But the revolution was both advancing and faltering as Luxemburg arrived in Berlin. On 9 November the Kaiser, who had fled to military headquarters in France, was persuaded that he no longer had the support of the army and agreed to abdicate in favour of his son, or grandson, or whoever was prepared to take the throne. In the centre of Berlin thousands of striking workers – called out by the USPD – mixed with soldiers, carrying red flags and demanding the Kaiser went. Prince Max informed Ebert of the Kaiser's decision and asked him whether he was prepared to take over as Imperial Chancellor. Ebert said he was. Scheidemann, hearing rumours that Liebknecht was about to proclaim a Socialist Republic, went to the Reichstag balcony at 2 p.m., announced that Ebert was now Chancellor, ending his speech, 'Long live the German Republic.' Ebert angrily told Scheidemann this had not been his intention. Whether Germany was to be a republic or a monarchy was for a constituent assembly to decide. Liebknecht, who had been driving around the city urging workers and soldiers to form councils, went to the Schloss, the royal palace, where a red flag was flying. At 4 p.m. he declared to the cheering faces below, 'I proclaim the free Socialist Republic of Germany … Those among you who want the world revolution, raise your hands to an oath.'[237] The crowd raised their hands.

An armed lorry of the Workers' and Soldiers' Council at the Brandenburg Gate in Berlin during the 1918 revolution.

That evening, the 9th, the Revolutionary Shop Stewards occupied the Reichstag and called on every Berlin factory and army regiment to form a council and send delegates – one for each thousand workers and for each battalion – to a conference the following day, a Sunday. The SPD, stronger and more effectively organised than the USPD and the Spartacists (who had no more than 50 members in Berlin), dominated the conference, calling for unity. Liebknecht was shouted down when he attacked the SPD. 'The counter-revolution is already underway. It is already in action. It is already among us.'[238] The conference agreed to government by a Council of People's Commissars comprising Ebert, Scheidemann and Otto Landsberg of the SPD and Hugo Haase, Wilhelm Dittmann and Emil Barth of the USPD. The Spartacists – who wanted authority to be with the workers' and soldiers' councils – criticised the agreement in a leaflet probably written by Luxemburg. *Nothing is gained by the fact that a few additional*

government Socialists have achieved power ... See to it that power, which
you have captured, does not slip out of your hands and that you use it for
your own good ... No co-operation with those who betrayed you for four
years.[239]

Ebert returned to his office at the Reich Chancellery. Later that
evening General Groener telephoned from army headquarters to
say that the High Command recognised his government. Ebert
asked what was expected of him. According to the transcript of
the conversation Groener said that Field Marshal von Hindenburg expected the government to support the officer corps in
maintaining military discipline. He went on, 'The officer corps
expects that the government will fight against Bolshevism and
places itself at the disposal of the government for such a purpose.'
Ebert asked Groener to pass his thanks to the Field Marshal.[240]
Ebert's dilemma was plain: securing the democratic republic the
SPD hoped for – as well as rebuilding the economy – depended
on the support of the most reactionary sections of German society,
the officer corps and the state bureaucracy, tying his government
to the imperial past. The alternative in his eyes was the disorder
the workers' councils would bring about, made manifest for him
in the famine and chaos now sweeping Bolshevik Russia.

On 11 November 1918 the war ended almost unnoticed as
Germany accepted the Allies' armistice terms. The following day
the Council of People's Commissars issued a manifesto setting
out a 'socialist programme' – elections to a constituent assembly
under proportional representation, freedom of the press and of
assembly, restoration of the pre-war labour laws and a promise
of welfare measures. But there were divisions, with the left of the
USPD pressing for a proletarian rather than bourgeois democratic
republic. Outside the government, the Spartacists were arguing

for rule by the workers' councils, with industry under the control of those who worked in it. On 15 November trade union leaders signed an agreement with the employers guaranteeing to maintain production, oppose nationalisation and undermine the councils.

Luxemburg and the Spartacist leaders stayed in the Hotel Excelsior for a week, their energies concentrated on finding premises in which to print *Red Flag*. On 11 November Luxemburg set out the League's immediate objectives: reissue the paper, produce a theoretical organ and special papers for young people, women and soldiers. According to Jacob, Luxemburg was besieged by visitors 'from all ranks of society, many of whom anticipated the Spartacists coming to power and scented advantages for themselves'.[241] It seems unlikely Luxemburg was in such demand given the Spartacus League's weakness and isolation, but Jacob gives a flavour of the party's more grandiose hopes. Luxemburg's life was confined to the small circle of Spartacus leaders and even Luise Kautsky, one of her closest pre-war friends, refused to meet her out of loyalty to her husband. *Red Flag* re-appeared on 18 November, Luxemburg sharing editorial responsibility with Liebknecht, but writing most of the leading articles, as well as overseeing layout and production.

The first article in *Red Flag*, 'The Beginning', described the achievements of the first week of revolution and what remained to be done. The Kaiser had been driven out, but the real enemy had always been capitalism, not monarchy. *A beginning has been made. What happens next is not in the hands of the dwarfs who would hold up the course of the revolution, who would put a spoke in the wheel of world history. It is the realisation of the ultimate goal of socialism which is on today's agenda of world history. The German revolution has now hit upon the path illuminated by this star. Step by step, through storm and stress, through battle and torment and misery and victory, it will reach its goal. It must!* Luxemburg had criticised the Bolsheviks for overturning the constituent assembly; now she denounced Ebert's promised constituent National Assembly, which she said was intended to create a *bourgeois counterweight to the workers' and soldiers' representatives … diverting the revolution on the track of a bourgeois revolution and spiriting it away from the socialist goals of the revolution.* She called for re-election of the workers' and soldiers' councils – which she knew were largely sympathetic to the SPD – and the raising of a Red Guard and workers' militia. *All power in the hands of the working masses, in the hands of the workers' and soldiers' councils, protection of the work of revolution against its lurking enemies – this is the guiding principle of all measures to be taken by the revolutionary government.*[242]

By 20 November Luxemburg was acknowledging that a National Assembly was likely, but what if it chose socialism? It would mean civil war. *For civil war is simply another name for class war, and the thought that socialism could be achieved without class war, that it follows from a mere majority resolution in parliament, is a ridiculous petit-bourgeois conception.* That sounded like civil war now or later. Luxemburg perhaps underestimated the effect of what she was saying on a population that, having endured four years of war and not seeing the subtlety of her words, might not take further death and misery so lightly. She raised the tempo a week later, saying, *The dwarfs who carry on their little games at the head of the revolution will either be thrown off the stage or they will finally learn to understand the colossal scale of the historical drama in which they are participating.*[243] Not that Liebknecht or Luxemburg themselves had any confidence in the councils as they were presently constituted. Liebknecht saw them as having 'very little enlightenment, very little class-consciousness', while Luxemburg wrote on 30 November that if the revolution depended on the councils it would be in dire straits.[244]

On 28 November the Hotel Excelsior management asked the Spartacists to leave. Luxemburg returned to her flat in Lindenstrasse, travelling from the suburbs to the *Red Flag* editorial office by train each day, arriving home after midnight. Jacob described

Luxemburg's happiness and satisfaction with the work she was doing. On one particular night Luxemburg stretched out in bed 'contentedly like a child', saying, *I shall sleep well. I have done everything that I wanted to do. I am so happy*.[245] But the journey from home to office became difficult and Luxemburg moved back into the centre, going from hotel to hotel, often asked to leave after one or two nights. While the conservative press denounced Luxemburg and Levi for their Jewish origins, the SPD's daily newspaper *Vörwarts* took a more proletarian tack, referring to, 'Karl Liebknecht, a certain Levi and the big-mouth Luxemburg, who never stood at a lathe or in a workshop, are in the process of ruining everything that we and our fathers aspired to.' A leaflet circulating in early December said, 'Judah has reached for the crown. We are to be ruled by Levi and Rosa Luxemburg.'[246] Luxemburg wrote to Sonia Liebknecht that while attacks on Jews had been ended in Russia, *I can imagine pogroms against Jews in Germany*.[247]

Confident in the army command's support, the government was now preparing its defences on the ground, a People's Naval Division and an armed SPD corps, and encouraging the growth of a para-military Freikorps of demobilised soldiers. The radicals could look to other soldiers returning home with their weapons and a force of trade union members under the control of the Berlin police commander Emil Eichhorn, a left-wing USPD supporter. The Spartacists had formed their own Red Soldiers' League. On 6 December soldiers occupied the *Red Flag* offices, alleging the Spartacists were planning a coup. In a day of confusion, forces loyal to the government killed 18 people at a demonstration organised by the Red Soldiers' League in Chausseestrasse. Over the next two days armed workers protected Spartacist demonstrations in Berlin. There were growing strikes and clashes throughout Germany, with radicals and SPD supporters charging one another with betraying the revolution. On 11 December columns of troops returning from France marched into Berlin, down the Unter den Linden to

'As you return unvanquished from the field of battle ...': the new Chancellor Friedrich Ebert welcoming troops home in Berlin on 11 December 1918.

the Brandenburg Gate. Ebert – who had lost two sons in the war – greeted them, 'As you return unvanquished from the field of battle ...'[248] Most had abandoned their regiments by nightfall.

At a USPD conference on 15 December the Spartacists demanded the USPD left the government. Luxemburg told the conference that in the five weeks since 9 November the forces of reaction had become stronger than they were on the first day of the revolution. The USPD leader Hugo Haase asked why the Spartacists did not follow their own logic and leave the USPD, whose delegates voted overwhelmingly for their representatives to remain in the government. The Spartacists were being outmanoeuvred and cut off. They demanded that a national congress of workers' and soldiers' councils convening in Berlin the next day should decide the form of Germany's government. The SPD called their bluff, *Vörwarts* declaring, 'All power to the Councils? All right then! They have recognised the Workers' and Soldiers' Councils as the highest power and will have to submit to [their] decision, whether they like it or not.'[249]

The national congress met from 16–20 December. The Spartacists had insisted that only workers who had jobs and soldiers should be allowed delegates' credentials. The congress, dominated by the SPD, took them at their word, refusing to allow Luxemburg and Liebknecht in. Luxemburg had written in *Red Flag* that the congress should reject proposals for a National Assembly, remove the Ebert government and form a Red Guard. But the delegates were decisively against the radicals, applauding the sponsor of the motion that the Council of People's Commissars should wield all executive power pending elections to the National Assembly on 19 January 1919. 'We Social Democrats must take at last a most decisive and persistent stand against the way in which our clean, clear, good Socialist ideology is constantly being sabotaged and discredited by Bolshevist perverseness.'[250] The delegates voted 344 to 98 in favour, in effect rejecting the Spartacists and the left of the USPD. But the delegates insisted that the Commissars should take the radical steps of removing officers' powers and nationalising the major industries. The government did neither.

Luxemburg recognised the blow the congress, the councils themselves, had struck at the Spartacists' hopes of a second revolutionary wave. She complained in *Red Flag* on 21 December that in past revolutionary clashes the forces and classes opposing one another had been clearly defined. *In the present revolution the defenders of the old order enter the lists not with the shields and coats of arms of the ruling classes, but under the banner of the 'Social Democratic Party'. If the cardinal question of the revolution was openly and honestly: capitalism or socialism, the great masses of the proletariat today would not have any doubts or hesitation about the answer.*[251] But this was the party Luxemburg had served from her arrival in Germany in 1898, as a rebel perhaps, but a rebel who said that even the worst workers' party was better than none. First the party and now the workers' councils had failed her.

∼

Luxemburg's exhaustion was beginning to tell. Walking from the *Red Flag* office one evening, she asked Jacob, *Can you tell me why I live constantly like this, without any inclination to do so? I would like to paint and live on a little plot of land where I can feed and love the animals. I would like to study natural science but above all else to live peacefully and on my own, not in this eternal whirlwind.* Jacob passed this on to Jogiches. 'Don't worry about it, Mathilde. If Rosa lived differently she would be even less satisfied. She *cannot* live differently.'[252] In another conversation, with Radek – whom Luxemburg and Jogiches had expelled from their party in 1912 and who arrived in Berlin on 20 December as Lenin's emissary – she raised her qualms about the terror the Bolsheviks were using against their opponents. Dzierzynski, another former member of the SDKPiL, was now head of the Russian secret police, the Cheka. When Liebknecht said he accepted revolutionary terror, Luxemburg asked how Dzierzynski could be so cruel. Radek noted that Jogiches laughed and said, 'If the need arises, you can do it too.'[253] Luxemburg's antagonism to Radek remained. Her first words to him on his arrival had been to tell him that the German revolution needed no Bolshevik commissar.

Ebert, though supported by the officers' corps and underpinned by the decision of the councils' congress, now feared for his control over the capital as the radical left rallied and what remained of the old army proved incapable of quelling disorder. On 24 December government troops fired on the People's Naval Division, who had shifted their allegiance to the USPD, following a dispute over wages in which the Division had taken an SPD military commander hostage and briefly besieged the Reich Chancellery. Armed workers, Spartacist supporters and police commandant Eichhorn's security force joined the battle, forcing the soldiers to back off. The SPD executive criticised Ebert's action and on 29 December the USPD withdrew its three representatives from the Council of People's Commissars in protest.

Luxemburg had returned to her flat on 24 December to celebrate Christmas Eve with Levi. On Christmas Day she wrote to Clara Zetkin in Stuttgart that 'official sources' had warned her not to sleep at home as there was a plot to assassinate her and Liebknecht. The SPD press was intensifying the campaign against the Spartacists, *Vörwarts* declaring, 'The shameless doings of Liebknecht and Luxemburg besmirch the revolution and endanger all its achievements.'[254] On 29 December Ebert appointed Noske as Defence Minister and instructed him to prepare the Freikorps to suppress the Spartacists, who were holding a conference that day at which they were expected to form a Communist Party.

The Spartacist League voted to sever its connection with the USPD, though Jogiches had advised against taking this step. On 30 December the conference reconvened, reinforced by delegates from radical left organisations in Bremen, Dresden and Hamburg, to form the Communist Party of Germany. The new party's problems began at once. Angered by a proposal to make Communist Party membership incompatible

> ### Freikorps
>
> Paramilitary organisations raised by former senior officers from demobilised soldiers to fill the vacuum in military force available to the Ebert government and the Weimar Republic. A unit mustered by General Georg von Maercker in December 1918, and inspected by Ebert and Noske in January 1919, set the model. The Freikorps were first deployed in the Spartacist rising and in March 1919 were dispatched to crush the Bavarian Socialist Republic. Up to 250,000 strong at their peak, the Freikorps were disbanded in April 1920. Many members went on to become Nazi Stormtroopers.

with trade union membership, the Revolutionary Shop Stewards withdrew, limiting any influence the party might have with the bulk of Berlin's industrial workers. Luxemburg, Liebknecht and Levi were prepared to contest elections to the National Assembly but were voted down by 62 votes to 23. Luxemburg's argument, that the Assembly – if it ever came about, and she had her doubts – would provide a forum for agitation, was ignored in the enthusiasm for action in the streets. A Marxist historian described most of the new party's members, not unfairly, as 'a rank-and-file composed largely of utopian radicals, quasi-anarchist or socially marginal elements ...'[255] Radek noted in his diary that he did not feel he was in the presence of a real party, while Luxemburg and Jogiches – who had been persistently outflanked by the politically more astute SPD and had now been overruled by their own members – sensed they had moved prematurely.

Luxemburg was at pains to make clear that the Communists would not, like the Bolsheviks, seize control through a coup. The party would only take power if that were the will of the majority of the working class, in Germany the majority of the population. Pale and exhausted, making her last public speech, she told the conference on 31 December that the revolution's second act was approaching. *Socialism cannot be created by decrees; nor can it be established by any government, however socialistic. Socialism must be created by the masses, by every proletarian. Where the chains of capitalism are forged, there they must be broken.* But when would the battle begin and how long would it take? *I make no attempt to prophesy how much time will be needed for this process. Who among us cares about time; who worries, so long only as our lives suffice to bring it to pass.*[256]

The government choreographed the next act. On 1 January 1919 an SPD newspaper accused Eichhorn, the Berlin police commander seen as over-sympathetic to the radicals, of embezzlement. He refused to relinquish his post when the government dismissed him on 4 January. That day Ebert and Noske inspected a parade of the newly-recruited Freikorps. 'Just be calm,' Noske told Ebert. 'Everything is going to be all right again.'[257] On 5 January the USPD and the Revolutionary Shop Stewards called a demonstration supporting Eichhorn, and were joined by the Communists. Impressed by the thousands of workers on the streets, delegates from the left of the USPD, the Shop Stewards and Liebknecht and Wilhelm Pieck from the Communists formed a provisional revolutionary committee to depose Ebert's government. Their supporters occupied buildings, including the offices of *Vörwarts*, in central Berlin. Neither Liebknecht nor Pieck had consulted the other Communist leaders. When Liebknecht returned to the party offices Luxemburg, realising the senselessness of a rising at this stage (as did Radek, who had more experience of what a coup involved), shouted at him, *Karl, what has happened to our programme?*[258] Noske moved the Freikorps into Berlin and a clash became inevitable.

But having condemned the rising, Luxemburg now took a dangerously ambiguous turn. On 7 January, rather than cooling passions as might have been expected, she wrote in *Red Flag*, *Disarm the counterrevolution, arm the masses, occupy all positions of power. Act quickly! The revolution obliges.*[259] The next day she said the masses would support revolutionary action if they had determined leadership. *The lesson of the last three days calls loudly to the leaders of the workers: do not talk, do not discuss endlessly, do not negotiate, act!*[260] That morning the Freikorps went into action against the radicals, beginning with a machine-gun assault on the *Red Flag* office. Luxemburg, constantly on the move, withdrew into herself, torn, one close to her believed, by internal conflict. Why had she acquiesced in and then encouraged a rising her intelligence opposed? Clara Zetkin said afterwards that Jogiches had explained that the Communist Party – he and Luxemburg – had been against the coup but could not desert the 'masses' in the midst of combat. 'Thus its role in the struggle had to be simultaneously negative-

Spartacist guards on the streets of Berlin, January 1919.

critical and positive-encouraging.'[261] This painfully over-intellec-
tualised explanation perhaps gives an insight into the basis of the
party's problems.

Luxemburg wrote to Zetkin on 11 January, *Right now the battle
is raging through Berlin, a lot of our brave boys have fallen*.[262] Jogiches
was arrested that day in the party office (though not recognised)
and a woman mistaken for Luxemburg badly beaten. Luxemburg
and Liebknecht moved to Neukölln, a working-class district,
moving again on 13 January, this time to Mannheimerstrasse
in the middle-class Wilmersdorf area. On 13 January *Vorwärts*
printed a poem regretting that while many workers were dying,
Luxemburg and Liebknecht were not with them in the mortuary.
The Freikorps were now mopping up the final doomed resistance
in bloody and pitiless street-fighting in which deaths rose to over
a thousand. Luxemburg, her cheeks sunken, her eyes dark with
tiredness, wrote her final article, 'Order reigns in Berlin'. *The leadership failed. But the leadership can and must be created anew by the*

masses and out of the masses … 'Order reigns in Berlin!' You stupid
lackeys! Your 'order' is built on sand. The revolution will 'raise itself
up again clashing', and to your horror it will proclaim to the sound of
trumpets: I was, I am, I shall be.[263]

~

On the evening of 15 January 1919 two men arrived at the house in
Mannheimerstrasse. Luxemburg, incapacitated by a headache, was
resting. The men brought her and Liebknecht together and asked
them to identify themselves. Both gave false names but there was
no difficulty in recognising them from photographs. Luxemburg
packed a small case with books and a change of clothes, expecting
another term of imprisonment. The two were taken in separate
cars to the Hotel Eden in Nurembergerstrasse, the headquarters
of the Garde-Kavallrie-Schutzendivision, a Freikorps unit that had
arrived in Berlin that day.

Luxemburg's car reached the hotel first at about 8.45 p.m.
Soldiers led her through the lobby, where others standing around
abused and taunted her. Captain Waldemar Pabst questioned
Luxemburg for a few minutes in his upstairs office, then ordered
Lieutenant Kurt Vogel to take her to Moabit Prison. Downstairs
an officer had instructed Otto Runge, a non-commissioned officer,
to shoot her when she re-appeared. He refused, fearing he might
injure people in the crowd gathering outside the building. As
Luxemburg stepped through the door, Vogel pushed her towards
Runge who hit her on the head and shoulder with the butt of his
rifle. She fell to the ground without a sound. She tried to stand
and Runge struck her again. Vogel and four soldiers dragged
Luxemburg, blood streaming from her nose and mouth, to the
waiting car and threw her into the back. As the car drew away,
Vogel stood on the running board and fired his revolver through
the open window. The bullet entered Luxemburg's left temple.

The car drove on to the River Spree. Soldiers pulled Luxemburg's body out and threw it into the river. Liebknecht had arrived at the hotel ten minutes after Luxemburg. He was hit with a rifle butt as he left the car and taken for interrogation by Pabst. As he left the building he was struck again, led to a car parked across the road and driven to the Tiergarten. The driver stopped, saying the engine had broken down. Liebknecht, semi-conscious, was forced onto the grass. Captain von Pflugk-Hartung killed him with a pistol. Soldiers bundled the body back into the car, returned to the city centre and dropped the corpse at a first-aid station as that of an 'unknown man'.

Jogiches, still unrecognised and freed the day after the murders, sent a telegram to Lenin saying simply, 'Rosa Luxemburg and Karl Liebknecht have carried out their ultimate revolutionary duty.'[264] In elections to the National Assembly two days later, boycotted by the Communists, the SPD won 37 per cent of the vote and the USPD 8 per cent. The SPD formed a coalition government with the Catholic Centre Party and the Democratic Party, with Scheidemann as Chancellor. Ebert became the Weimar Republic's first President. On 25 January Liebknecht was buried at the Friedrichsfelde cemetery with other victims of the January fighting. An empty coffin representing Luxemburg was buried alongside. Jogiches told Jacob, 'I hope her little body will be found.'[265] Jogiches investigated the murders and on 12 February *Red Flag* published a detailed and largely accurate description of the night's events. Jogiches was arrested on 10 March and this time identified. He was taken to a room where Freikorps officers were waiting, tortured and then shot 'while trying to escape'.

On 31 May a passer-by saw a body against sluice gates in the Landwehr Canal in Berlin, Luxemburg's remains. Noske, Defence Minister in the new government, ordered the removal of the corpse to a military camp outside Berlin for secret burial. When the press revealed his plan, Luxemburg's friends insisted they be allowed

Rosa Luxemburg's funeral at the Friedrichsfelde cemetery in Berlin, 13 June 1919.

to arrange her funeral. Jacob paid three marks for the body to be released from the mortuary, identifying Luxemburg from what was left of her velvet dress, a gold charm and a pair of gloves she had bought her. On 13 June a hearse took Luxemburg's coffin from Südende to the Friedrichsfelde cemetery, followed by workers and uniformed soldiers and sailors carrying banners and red flags. Levi – now Communist Party leader – spoke first at the graveside, followed by Clara Zetkin. Levi looked forward to the triumph of the revolution. 'And in that hour of victory we shall have once again to look back on all of those who have lived for us and have died for us. Indeed, they all died with that hour in mind.'[266] As the red flags were lowered over Luxemburg's grave the mourners sang the revolutionary hymn, the Internationale.

Notes

1. Paul Frölich, *Rosa Luxemburg* (Pluto Press & Bookmarks, London: 1994) p 23, hereafter Frölich.
2. Richard Abraham, *Rosa Luxemburg: A Life for the International* (Berg, Oxford, New York and Munich: 1989) p 23, hereafter Abraham.
3. Luise Kautsky, 'Remembering Rosa Luxemburg', in Paul Le Blanc, *Rosa Luxemburg: Reflections and Writings* (Humanity Books, Amherst, New York: 1999) p 34, hereafter Luise Kautsky.
4. 24 June 1898, Elzbieta Ettinger (ed. & trans.), *Comrade and Lover, Rosa Luxemburg's Letters to Leo Jogiches* (Pluto Press, London: 1979) p 47, hereafter *Comrade and Lover*.
5. 20 April 1900, Elzbieta Ettinger, *Rosa Luxemburg A Life* (Beacon Press, Boston, Mass.: 1986) p 105, hereafter Ettinger.
6. Ettinger, p 11.
7. *Comrade and Lover*, pp 1–2.
8. Ettinger, p 27.
9. Richard Pipes, *Communism A Brief History* (Weidenfeld & Nicolson, London: 2001) p 8, hereafter Pipes.
10. Karl Marx and Friedrich Engels (trans. Samuel Moore), *The Communist Manifesto* (The Merlin Press, London: 1998) pp 3, 11, 30, hereafter *The Communist Manifesto*.
11. *The Communist Manifesto*, p 18.

12. Meghnad Desai, *Marx's Revenge: The Resurgence of Capitalism and the Death of Statist Socialism* (Verso, London and New York: 2004) p 10, hereafter Desai.

13. Karl Marx, *Contribution to the Critique of Political Economy*, quoted Desai, p 44.

14. Stephen Eric Bronner, *Rosa Luxemburg A Revolutionary for Our Times* (Pennsylvania State University Press, University Park, Pennsylvania: 1987) p 85.

15. Frölich, p 29.

16. *Comrade and Lover*, p xix.

17. J P Nettl, *Rosa Luxemburg* (Oxford University Press, Oxford and London: 1966, two volumes) Vol 1, p 64, hereafter Nettl.

18. 14 September 1899, *Comrade and Lover*, p 19.

19. Luise Kautsky, pp 35, 48.

20. Description by John Mill, Nettl Vol 1, p 83.

21. Nettl Vol 2, p 674.

22. Ettinger, p 90.

23. Ettinger, pp 45, 55.

24. *Comrade and Lover*, p ix–xx.

25. Sam Dolgoff (ed.), *Bakunin on Anarchism* (Black Rose Books, Montreal: 1980) p 295.

26. Donald Sassoon, *One Hundred Years of Socialism: The West European Left in the Twentieth Century* (I B Tauris, London: 1996) p xx.

27. Frölich, p 38.

28. Nettl Vol 1, p 73.

29. 25 March 1894, *Comrade and Lover*, pp 8, 12.

30. 21 March 1895, *Comrade and Lover*, p 17.

31. 28 March 1895, *Comrade and Lover*, pp 21–2.

32. 5 March 1896, in Stephen Eric Bronner (ed,), *The Letters of Rosa Luxemburg* (Westview Press, Boulder, Colorado: 1978) p 59, hereafter Bronner, *Letters*.

33. Nettl Vol 1, pp 74, 76.
34. Ettinger, p 105.
35. 12 July 1896, *Comrade and Lover*, p 27.
36. Ettinger, p 67.
37. 16 July 1897, *Comrade and Lover*, pp 22, 23–4.
38. Ettinger, p 68.
39. 12 July 1896, *Comrade and Lover*, p 27.
40. March 1898, Nettl Vol 1, p 144.
41. Ettinger, p 93.
42. Lucien Laurat, *Marxism and Democracy* (Victor Gollancz, London: 1940) pp 53–4.
43. Nettl Vol 1, p 121.
44. Richard J Evans (ed.), *The German Working Class 1888–1933: The Politics of Everyday Life* (Croom Helm, London; Barnes & Noble Books, Totowa, New Jersey: 1982) pp 19–20.
45. David McLellan, *Karl Marx: Interviews and Recollections* (Macmillan, London: 1981) p 153.
46. Richard M Watt, *The Kings Depart, The Tragedy of Germany: Versailles and the German Revolution* (Phoenix, London: 2003) p 113, hereafter Watt.
47. Desai, p 106.
48. 24 June 1898, *Comrade and Lover*, p 47.
49. 17 May 1898, *Comrade and Lover*, pp 33–5.
50. 30 May 1898, Nettl Vol 1, p 131.
51. Ettinger, pp 80–1.
52. 30 December 1899, Bronner, *Letters*, p 79.
53. 24 June 1898, *Comrade and Lover*, p 44.
54. 24 June 1898, *Comrade and Lover*, p 48.
55. Ettinger, p 79.
56. H Tudor and J M Tudor (eds), *Marxism and Social Democracy: The Revisionist Debate 1896–1898* (Cambridge

University Press, Cambridge: 1988) pp 222, 168–9, hereafter Tudors.

57. 2 July 1898, *Comrade and Lover*, p 53.

58. Peter Hudis and Kevin B Anderson, *The Rosa Luxemburg Reader* (Monthly Review Press, New York: 2004) p 426, hereafter *RLR*.

59. Rosa Luxemburg, *Social Reform or Revolution*, in *RLR*, pp 129, 133–4, hereafter *Social Reform or Revolution*.

60. *Social Reform or Revolution*, p 156.

61. 2 September 1898, *Comrade and Lover*, p 62.

62. 3 November 1898, Nettl Vol. 1, p 159.

63. Tudors, pp 281, 284.

64. 2 September 1898, *Comrade and Lover*, p 66.

65. Werner Thönnessen, *The Emancipation of Women: The Rise and Decline of the Women's Movement in German Social Democracy 1863–1933* (Pluto Press, London: 1973) p 67, hereafter Thönnessen.

66. Abraham, p 55.

67. Mathilde Jacob, *Rosa Luxemburg, An Intimate Portrait* (trans. Hans Fernbach) (Lawrence & Wishart, London: 2000) p 37, hereafter Jacob.

68. Nettl Vol 1, p 193.

69. *Die Gleichheit* No 18 (1892), in Thönnessen, p 163.

70. Rosa Luxemburg, 'The Proletarian Woman', in *RLR*, p 245.

71. Beatrice Farnsworth, *Aleksandra Kollontai: Socialism, Feminism and the Bolshevik Revolution* (Stanford University Press, Stanford, CA: 1980) p 45.

72. Rosa Luxemburg, 'Address to the 1907 International Socialist Women's Conference', in *RLR*, p 240.

73. Rosa Luxemburg, 'Women's suffrage and class struggle', in *RLR*, p 242.

74. Luise Kautsky, pp 44, 45.

75. Ettinger, p 86.
76. 5 December 1899, *Comrade and Lover*, p 110.
77. 6 March 1899, *Comrade and Lover*, p 73.
78. Ettinger, p 85.
79. Frölich, p 80.
80. 30 April 1900, *Comrade and Lover*, p 98.
81. Nettl Vol 2, p 675.
82. 27 August 1917, Bronner, *Letters*, p 227.
83. Ettinger, p 109.
84. 28 January 1902, *Comrade and Lover*, p 122.
85. 20 February 1902, *Comrade and Lover*, p 129.
86. Nettl Vol 1, p 188.
87. 27 September 1902, Bronner, *Letters*, p 91.
88. 11 October 1902, Bronner, *Letters*, pp 91–2.
89. Ettinger, p 113.
90. V I Lenin, *What Is To Be Done, Burning Questions of Our Movement* (Foreign Languages Press, Peking: 1973) p 37.
91. Ettinger, p 119.
92. Rosa Luxemburg, *Organisational Questions of Russian Social Democracy*, in *RLR*, p 252, hereafter *Organisational Questions*.
93. *Organisational Questions*, pp 253–4.
94. *Organisational Questions*, pp 261, 265.
95. John H Kautsky, *Karl Kautsky: Marxism, Revolution and Democracy* (Transaction Publishers, New Brunswick & London: 1994) p 55.
96. Ernest Mandel, quoted in Paul Le Blanc, *Rosa Luxemburg: Reflections and Writings* (Humanity Books, Amherst, New York: 1999) p 83, hereafter Le Blanc.
97. Marshall S Shatz, *Jan Waclaw Machajski: A Radical Critic of the Russian Intelligentsia* (University of Pittsburg Press, Pittsburg: 1989).
98. *Social Reform or Revolution*, p 130.

99. Rosa Luxemburg, *What does the Spartacus League want?*, in *RLR*, pp 346, 350, hereafter *What does the Spartacist League want?*

100. Rosa Luxemburg, *The Socialisation of Society*, in *RLR*, p 348, hereafter *Socialisation of Society*.

101. *Socialisation of Society*, pp 346–7.

102. *Socialisation of Society*, p 348.

103. *What does the Spartacus League want?*, pp 356–7.

104. *What does the Spartacist League want?*, p 357.

105. Watt, p 116; Bronner, *Letters*, p 94.

106. Frölich, p 91.

107. *Comrade and Lover*, pp 137, 139.

108. Nettl Vol 1, p 198.

109. Frölich, p 94.

110. Bronner, *Letters*, p 97.

111. *Comrade and Lover*, pp 145, 147.

112. 20 October 1905, *Comrade and Lover*, p 153.

113. Nettl Vol 1, pp 17–18.

114. Ettinger, p 160.

115. *Socialisation of Society*, p 347.

116. Frölich, p 149.

117. Frölich, p 112.

118. 3 November 1905, *Comrade and Lover*, pp 155–6.

119. Frölich, p 113.

120. Bronner, *Letters*, p 100.

121. Frölich, p 114.

122. Ettinger, p 132.

123. Frölich, pp 126–7.

124. Raya Dunayevskaya, *Rosa Luxemburg, Women's Liberation, and Marx's Philosophy of Revolution* (Humanities Press, New Jersey; Harvest Press, Sussex: 1981) p 47, hereafter Dunayevskaya.

125. Ettinger, p 138.

126. Nettl Vol 1, p 368.
127. *What does the Spartacus League want?*, p 363.
128. Rosa Luxemburg, *The Mass Strike, the Political Party, and the Trade Unions*, in *RLR*, pp 170, 171, hereafter *The Mass Strike*.
129. *The Mass Strike*, pp 182, 186.
130. *The Mass Strike*, p 199.
131. Ettinger, p 172.
132. Rosa Luxemburg, *The Russian Revolution*, in *RLR*, p 283.
133. Luise Kautsky, p 38.
134. 5 January 1899, Dunayevskaya, p 5.
135. Nettl Vol 1, p 408.
136. Frölich, p 192.
137. Bronner, *Letters*, pp 121–2.
138. Nettl Vol 1, p 383.
139. Nettl Vol 1, p 17.
140. Abraham, p 87.
141. Leon Trotsky, *My Life: An Attempt at an Autobiography* (Pathfinder, London: 1970) p 157, hereafter Trotsky.
142. Rosa Luxemburg, 'Address to the 1907 International Socialist Women's Conference', in *RLR*, pp 236–7.
143. Frölich, p 178.
144. Rosa Luxemburg, *The National Question and Autonomy*, in Le Blanc, pp 129, 136–7.
145. Nettl Vol 1, p 390.
146. Luise Kautsky, p 49.
147. September 1909, *Comrade and Lover*, p 171.
148. 20 March 1907, in *RLR*, p 13.
149. Norman Geras, *The Legacy of Rosa Luxemburg* (New Left Books, London: 1976) p 36.
150. Trotsky, p 166.
151. 7 March, 17 March 1910, Bronner, *Letters*, p 132.

152. Rosa Luxemburg, *Theory and Practice*, in *RLR*, p 209, hereafter *Theory and Practice*.

153. Nettl Vol 1, pp 387–8; Vol 2, p 490.

154. 13 April 1910, Bronner, *Letters*, p 133.

155. *Theory and Practice*, p 171.

156. 5 August 1910, *Comrade and Lover*, p 176.

157. Nettl Vol 1, p 433.

158. Dunayevskaya, p 27; Nettl Vol 1, p 432.

159. 23 September 1910, *Comrade and Lover*, pp 176–7.

160. Dunayevskaya, p 61.

161. Dunayevskaya, p 25.

162. Dunayevskaya, p 26.

163. Ettinger, p 174.

164. 12 May 1917, Bronner, *Letters*, pp 204, 205–6.

165. August 1912, *Comrade and Lover*, pp 180–1.

166. Nettl Vol 2, p 471.

167. Ettinger, p 175.

168. Watt, p 127.

169. Norman Geras, 'Rosa Luxemburg: Barbarism and the Collapse of Capitalism', *New Left Review* 82 (November-December 1973).

170. *Social Reform or Revolution*, p 132.

171. 12 May 1917, Bronner, *Letters*, p 204.

172. Frölich, p 169.

173. Rosa Luxemburg, *The Accumulation of Capital: An Anti-Critique*, in Le Blanc, p 177.

174. Abraham, pp 111–12.

175. Jacob, pp 24–5.

176. Frölich, p 154.

177. Frölich, p 185.

178. Nettl Vol 2, pp 481, 490.

179. Frölich, p 186.

180. 11 March 1914, Bronner, *Letters*, p 153. The recipient of the letter, Walter Stöcker, subsequently died in a Nazi concentration camp.
181. Ettinger, p 188.
182. 7 January 1917, Bronner, *Letters*, p 176.
183. Frölich, p 193.
184. David Fernbach, 'Rosa Luxemburg's Political Heir: An Appreciation of Paul Levi', in *New Left Review* 238 (November–December 1999).
185. Hew Strachan, *The First World War, Volume 1: To Arms* (Oxford University Press, Oxford) p 121, hereafter Strachan; Nettl Vol 2, p 604.
186. Strachan, pp 121–2.
187. Watt, p 118.
188. Strachan, p 1134.
189. Frölich p 115.
190. Rosa Luxemburg, *Rebuilding the International*, in Le Blanc, pp 200, 210.
191. Abraham, p 119.
192. Ettinger, p 195.
193. Bronner, *Letters*, p 156.
194. *Rebuilding the International*, in Le Blanc, pp 203–4.
195. 23 February 1915, Frölich, p 221.
196. Jacob, p 32.
197. 12 March 1915, Bronner, *Letters*, p 161.
198. Jacob, p 39.
199. Rosa Luxemburg, *The Crisis in Social Democracy* ('The Junius Pamphlet'), in *RLR*, p 313, hereafter Junius Pamphlet.
200. Junius Pamphlet, pp 327, 340–1, 321.
201. Nettl Vol 2, pp 640–1.
202. Jacob, pp 37, 38.
203. Jacob, p 46.
204. Frölich, p 232.

205. 7 July 1916, Bronner, *Letters*, p 168.
206. 23 May 1917, Bronner, *Letters*, p 209.
207. 29 June 1917, Ettinger, p 209. The building subsequently became the headquarters of the Gestapo.
208. Jacob, p 62.
209. Nettl Vol 2, p 665.
210. 16 February 1917, Lelio Basso, *Rosa Luxemburg: A Reappraisal* (Andre Deutsch, London: 1975) p 172.
211. Strachan, p 1005.
212. 7 January 1917, Bronner, *Letters*, p 174.
213. Ettinger, p 215.
214. Jacob, p 61.
215. 28 December 1916, Bronner, *Letters*, pp 661–2.
216. 16 February 1917, Nettl Vol 2, p 663.
217. Ettinger, p 222.
218. 23 May 1917, Bronner, *Letters*, p 209.
219. 1 June 1917, Nettl Vol 2, p 666.
220. Jacob, pp 66, 87.
221. Nettl Vol 2, p 674.
222. Mid-November 1917, Bronner, *Letters*, p 235.
223. Chris Harman, *The Lost Revolution, Germany 1918 to 1923* (Bookmarks, London: 1997 rev. ed.) p 11, hereafter Harman.
224. Nettl Vol 2, p 689.
225. Ettinger, p 224.
226. Rosa Luxemburg, *The Russian Revolution*, in *RLR*, p 284, hereafter *Russian Revolution*.
227. *Russian Revolution*, p 305.
228. *Russian Revolution*, p 307.
229. Nettl Vol 1, p 3.
230. Frölich, p 260.
231. Nettl Vol 2, pp 708–9.
232. Frölich, p 262.

233. Watt, p 183.

234. Frölich, p 265.

235. Jacob, p 93.

236. *Russian Revolution*, p 287.

237. Watt, p 198.

238. Harman, p 48.

239. Nettl Vol 2, p 719.

240. Watt, p 200.

241. Jacob, p 94.

242. Rosa Luxemburg, 'The Beginning', in *RLR*, pp 344, 345, 343.

243. *Red Flag* 20 and 27 November 1918, Nettl Vol 2, pp 726–7, 733.

244. Sebastian Haffner, *Failure of a Revolution: Germany 1918–19* (Andre Deutsch, London: 1973) p 109, hereafter Haffner.

245. Jacob, p 95.

246. David Fernbach, 'Rosa Luxemburg's Political Heir: An Appreciation of Paul Levi', in *New Left Review* 238 (November-December 1999).

247. Ettinger, p 238.

248. Watt, p 211.

249. *Vörwarts*, 16 December 1918, Nettl Vol 2, p 743.

250. Werner T Angress, *Stillborn Revolution: The Communist Bid for Power in Germany, 1921–1923* (Princeton University Press, Princeton NJ: 1963) p 19, hereafter Angress.

251. *Red Flag* 21 December 1918, Frölich pp 281–2.

252. Jacob, p 97.

253. Nettl Vol 2, p 731.

254. Frölich, p 290.

255. Eric Hobsbawm, 'Confronting Defeat: The German Communist Party', in *New Left Review* 61 (May-June 1970).

256. Rosa Luxemburg, 'Our Programme and the Political Situation', in *RLR*, pp 368, 373.

257. Harman, p 60.

258. Haffner, p 137.

259. *Red Flag* 7 January 1919, in Le Blanc, p 268.

260. *Red Flag* 8 January 1919, Nettl Vol 2, p 765.

261. Angress, pp 30–1.

262. 11 January 1919, Nettl Vol 2, p 759.

263. *Red Flag* 14 January 1919, in *RLR*, p 378.

264. Nettl Vol 2, p 779.

265. Jacob, p 102.

266. Memorial speech by Paul Levi, in Jacob, p 123.

Year	Age	Life
1871		5 March: Born Rozalia Luksenburg in Zamosc, Russian-occupied Poland.
1873	2	Family moves to Warsaw.
1876	5	Suffers hip condition, leaving her disabled for life.
1881	10	Starts at Russian Second High School for Girls.
1887	16	Graduates from the High School; active in underground socialist group.
1889	18	Moves to Switzerland; registers at Zurich University as Rosa Luxemburg; meets Russian socialist exiles.
1890	19	Meets Leo Jogiches, a Lithuanian socialist with whom she has a long-term personal and political relationship.
1893	22	Addresses Socialist International congress for the first time.
1894	23	Studies in Paris; writes programme for Social Democracy of the Kingdom of Poland (SDKP), which she establishes with Jogiches, Julian Marchlewski and Adolf Warski.
1896	25	First article published by German Social Democrats (SPD) theoretical journal *Die Neue Zeit*; speaks at Socialist International congress in London, SDKP recognised by the International.
1897	26	Awarded doctorate for thesis *The Industrial Development of Poland*; mother dies in Warsaw.

Year	History	Culture
1871	Wilhelm I of Prussia declared German Emperor at Versailles. The Paris Commune.	Lewis Carroll, *Alice Through the Looking Glass*. Charles Darwin, *The Descent of Man*.
1873	Death of Napoleon III. German forces leave France.	Walter Pater, *Studies in the History of the Renaissance*.
1876	Ottoman Sultan deposed.	Henry James, *Roderick Hudson*. Wagner, *Siegfried*.
1881	First Boer War. Persecution of Jews in Russia.	Pablo Picasso born.
1887	Queen Victoria's Golden Jubilee.	Conan Doyle, *A Study in Scarlet*.
1889	Suicide of Austrian Crown Prince at Mayerling. Birth of Adolf Hitler.	Jerome K Jerome, *Three Men in a Boat*.
1890	Bismarck dismissed by Kaiser Wilhelm II. German SDP adopt Marxist Erfurt Programme.	Ibsen, *Hedda Gabler*.
1893	Formation of Independent Labour Party in Britain. Franco-Russian alliance signed.	Tchaikovsky, 'Pathetique' symphony.
1894	Sino-Japanese War begins. Tsar Nicholas II accedes to the throne of Russia.	Grossmith, *Diary of a Nobody*. Rudyard Kipling, *The Jungle Book*.
1896	Nobel Prizes established. Italian army defeated by Abyssinians at Adowa.	Chekov, *The Seagull*.
1897	Turkey defeated in war with Greece. Russia occupies Port Arthur in China.	H G Wells, *The Invisible Man*.

Year	Age	Life
1898	27	Marries Gustav Lübeck to obtain German citizenship; moves to Berlin and joins SPD; addresses Reichstag election rallies in Upper Silesia; articles published in *Leipziger Volkszeitung* attacking Bernstein's 'revisionism'; addresses SPD congress on issue; edits *Sächsiche Arbeiterzeitung* for short period; meets SPD women's activist Clara Zetkin.
1899	28	Articles on revisionism published as *Social Reform or Revolution*; her social circle in Berlin includes the influential party couples the Kautskys, the Bebels, the Eisners and the Mehrings; refuses offer of editorial post at SPD paper *Vörwarts*.
1900	29	Jogiches moves to Berlin from Switzerland after much urging; attends Socialist International congress in Paris; father dies in Warsaw; moribund SDKP enlarged to form the Socialist Democracy of the Kingdom of Poland and Lithuania (SDKPiL)
1902	31	Becomes contributing editor at the *Leipziger Volkszeitung* but resigns after clashes with Mehring; writes bulk of articles in short-lived SDKPiL paper, the *People's Gazette*.
1903	32	Becomes sole woman member of the International Socialist Bureau; addresses Reichstag election rallies in Upper Silesia; marriage with Lübeck dissolved.
1904	33	Writes *Organisational Questions of Russian Social Democracy* criticising Lenin's centralist party organisation; attends Socialist International Congress in Amsterdam as SPD and SDKPiL delegate; sentenced to three months' imprisonment for insulting the Kaiser in 1903 election campaign.

Year	History	Culture
1898	Kitchener defeats Sudanese at Omdurman. Spanish-American war. Kaiser Wilhelm II visits Palestine and Syria.	H G Wells, *The War of the Worlds*. Oscar Wilde, *The Ballad of Reading Gaol*.
1899	Second Boer War begins. First Peace Conference at the Hague. Germany secures Baghdad railway contract.	Elgar, 'Enigma Variations'.
1900	Second Boer War: British relieve Ladysmith and Mafeking. Bernard von Bulow named German Chancellor.	Joseph Conrad, *Lord Jim*.
1902	Second Boer War ends. Triple Alliance between Germany, Austria and Italy renewed for another 6 years. Trotsky escapes from Siberia and settles in London.	A E W Mason, *The Four Feathers*.
1903	Anglo-French 'Entente Cordiale' formed.	Jack London, *The Call of the Wild*.
33	Russo-Japanese War begins. Assassination of Plehve. Revolt in German SW Africa.	G K Chesterton, *The Napoleon of Notting Hill*. Puccini, 'Madame Butterfly'.

Year	Age	Life
1905	34	Visits Jogiches briefly in Cracow, where he has gone to organise SDKPiL activities in Russian revolution; tells him she has been involved with another man; calls on SPD at congress in Jena to take up mass strike tactic; becomes an associate editor of *Vörwarts*; returns to Warsaw as the revolution is subsiding.
1906	35	Arrested in Warsaw with Jogiches; allowed bail on health grounds after four months, fails to return for trial; goes to St Petersburg and then to Finland where she writes *The Mass Strike, the Political Party, and the Trade Unions*; begins affair with Konstantin (Costia) Zetkin.
1907	36	Addresses rallies in Reichstag election campaign; ends relationship with Jogiches, though they remain close political allies; both attend Russian Social Democratic Labour Party (RSDLP) congress; imprisoned for two months for incitement to violence; co-operates with Bolsheviks and Mensheviks on anti-war resolution at Socialist International congress in Amsterdam; criticises Lenin's national self-determination policy in SDKPiL's *Social Democratic Review*; becomes lecturer at SPD school.
1909	38	Relationship with Costia Zetkin falters.
1910	39	Bitter dispute with Kautsky over the SPD's direction and his commitment to parliamentary democracy; takes leave from SPD school for agitational speaking tour; isolated at SPD congress in Magdeburg.

Year	History	Culture
1905	Russian defeat in war with Japan; 'Bloody Sunday' massacre in St Petersburg; general strike in Russia and formation of Workers' Soviet; Tsar concedes reforms. Tangier Crisis: threat of European war over Morocco.	Cézanne, 'Les Grandes Baigneuses'.
1906	Algeciras Conference gives France and Spain control of Morocco. Russian parliament (the Duma) dissolved after two months. Nansen traverses the North-West Passage. HMS *Dreadnought* launched.	Birth of Dmitri Shostakovich.
1907	Second Russian Duma meets. Hague Peace Conference. Lenin leaves Russia and founds newspaper 'The Proletarian'.	Joseph Conrad, *The Secret Agent*. Rudyard Kipling wins Nobel Prize for Literature.
1909	Young Turk revolt overthrows Turkish sultan. Anglo-German discussions on control of Baghdad railway.	Diaghilev presents his 'Ballets Russe' for the first time.
1910	Death of King Edward VII: accession of George V. Revolution in Portugal: republic declared.	E M Forster, *Howard's End*. Stravinsky, 'The Firebird'.

Year	Age	Life
1911	40	Criticised by SPD for revealing confidential party document on Morocco crisis; denounces party acquiescence in German government's aggressive foreign policy; SDKPiL splits between activists in Warsaw and leadership in Berlin.
1912	41	Part of loose left-wing alliance in SPD; addresses rallies in Reichstag election campaign; writes *The Accumulation of Capital: A Contribution to the Economic Explanation of Capitalism*.
1913	42	Defeated on issues of SPD support for increased arms spending and mass strikes at party congress in Jena; helps establish *Socialdemocratische Korrespondenz* to press left-wing argument in SPD.
1914	43	Sentenced to a year's imprisonment for incitement to disobedience but freed pending appeal; speech from dock published as *Militarism, War and the Working Class*; begins affair with defence lawyer Paul Levi; attacks army in *Socialdemocratische Korrespondenz* for ill-treating conscripts but subsequent trial for insulting the military is aborted by authorities; attends emergency Socialist International congress on eve of First World War; close to suicide when SPD supports war; forms anti-war International Group with Liebknecht, Mehring and Zetkin.

Year	History	Culture
1911	National Insurance Bill introduced in British Parliament. Coronation of King George V. Agadir Crisis. Russian premier Stolypin assassinated. Nationalist revolution in China. Roald Amundsen reaches the South Pole.	Rupert Brooke, *Poems*. Strauss, 'Der Rosenkavalier'.
1912	British coal, transport and London dock workers strike. First Balkan War. Triple Alliance of Germany, Austria and Italy renewed. Lenin takes over editorship of *Pravda*. Sinking of the *Titanic*.	Picasso, 'The Violin'.
1913	Suffragette demonstrations in London. Second Balkan War. Ebert becomes leader of German SPD.	D H Lawrence, *Sons and Lovers*. Thomas Mann, *Death in Venice*.
43	Assassination of Archduke Franz Ferdinand at Sarajevo. Outbreak of First World War. Western Front: battle of the Marne prevents German army taking Paris. Trench warfare begins; first battle of Ypres. Eastern Front: Germans under Hindenburg defeat Russian armies at Tannenberg and Masurian Lakes in East Prussia.	James Joyce, *Dubliners*. Edgar Rice Burroughs, *Tarzan of the Apes*.

Year	Age	Life
1915	44	Begins serving sentence at Barnimstrasse Prison; writes *Anti-Critique*, a response to criticisms of *The Accumulation of Capital*, and *The Crisis of Social Democracy* under the pen-name Junius; drafts the Spartacus League's guiding principles.
1916	45	Released from prison, continues anti-war activities including May Day demonstration at which Karl Liebknecht is arrested; re-arrested and placed in preventive custody at Barnimstrasse and then Wronke in German Poland; writes articles for Spartacus Letters; opposes Independent Socialist Party (USPD) break with SPD but agrees to attach Spartacus League to USPD.
1917	46	Friends' attempts to secure release on health grounds fail; transferred to Breslau Prison; supports Bolshevik coup in Russia but writes prophetic criticisms in *The Russian Revolution*.

Year	History	Culture
44	First World War. Western Front: Battles of Neuve Chapelle and Loos. Eastern Front: Germans take Warsaw and Brest-Litovsk. Gallipoli campaign. First Zeppelin air raids on London. At sea: First U-boat campaign against Allied shipping; Battle of Dogger Bank.	D H Lawrence, *The Rainbow*. W Somerset Maugham, *Of Human Bondage*. Death of Rupert Brooke
45	First World War. Western Front: Germans attack at Verdun; Battle of the Somme. Hindenburg becomes Chief of the General Staff. Eastern Front: Brusilov offensive by Russians. At sea: the Battle of Jutland.	James Joyce, *Portrait of the Artist as a Young Man*. Film: D W Griffiths' *Intolerance*.
46	First World War. Western Front: Battle of Passchendale; battle of Cambrai. Eastern Front: Tsar overthrown in February Revolution; Provisional Government removed in Bolshevik October Revolution; new government signs armistice with Germany. German unrestricted U-boat warfare brings USA into war on Allied side.	First jazz recordings made.

Year	Age	Life
1918	47	Freed in November Revolution; returns to Berlin to revive Spartacus League with Jogiches and Liebknecht and edit newspaper *Die Rote Fahne* ('The Red Flag'); writes *The Socialisation of Society*, *What does the Spartacus League want?* and numerous agitational articles; founder leader of the Communist Party of Germany.
1919	47	15 January: Murdered with Liebknecht by Freikorps following suppression of Spartacist rising, which she had opposed; her last article is *Order Prevails in Berlin*; her body is found in River Spree five months after her death.

Year	History	Culture
47	First World War. Eastern Front: Treaty of Brest-Litovsk brings major gains for Germany. Western Front: German March offensive defeated; Allied offensive in autumn breaks through German lines: armistice signed 11 November 1918. Kaiser abdicates and republic declared.	Lytton Strachey, *Eminent Victorians*.
47	Peace conference opens at Versailles	Thomas Hardy, *Collected Poems*.

Further Reading

The major biography of Luxemburg is J P Nettl's two-volume *Rosa Luxemburg* (Oxford University Press, London and New York: 1966). An abridged version was published in 1989. Elzbieta Ettinger's *Rosa Luxemburg, A Life* (Beacon Press, Boston, Mass.: 1986) has the advantage of newer material but is at times over-imaginative. A longstanding work is Paul Frölich (trans. Joanna Hoornweg), *Rosa Luxemburg: Ideas in Action* (Pluto Press/Bookmarks, London: 1994). First published in 1940, this biographer had the advantage of knowing Luxemburg, as did Mathilde Jacob, whose *Rosa Luxemburg, An Intimate Portrait* (Lawrence & Wishart/Heretic Books, London: 2000, translated by Hans Fernbach) is sentimental in parts but full of interesting personal detail.

Among other books on Luxemburg's life and ideas worth looking at are Stephen Eric Bronner, *Rosa Luxemburg, A Revolutionary for Our Times* (Pennsylvania State University Press: University Park, Pennsylvania 1997), which takes a thematic approach, Richard Abraham, *Rosa Luxemburg: A Life for the International* (Berg, Oxford, New York and Munich: 1989), and Norman Geras, *The Legacy of Rosa Luxemburg* (New Left Books, London: 1976). Much of Luxemburg's thoughts and feelings can be followed in her letters. The most interesting collections are Stephen Eric Bronner (ed.), *The Letters of Rosa Luxemburg* (Westview Press, Boulder, Colorado: 1978) and Elzbieta Ettinger (ed. and trans.) *Comrade and Lover, Rosa Luxemburg's Letters to Leo Jogiches* (Pluto Press, London: 1979).

There are a number of collections of Luxemburg's principal writing. The most recent is Helen Scott (ed.), *The Essential Rosa Luxemburg – Reform or Revolution and the Mass Strike* (Haymarket Books, Chicago: 2007). The doughty will also want to see Rosa Luxemburg, *The Accumulation of Capital* (Routledge, London: 2003). There is a wide-ranging anthology (and an excellent introduction) in Peter Hudis and Kevin B Anderson (eds), *The Rosa Luxemburg Reader* (Monthly Review Press, New York: 2004). Useful extracts can be found in Paul Le Blanc (ed.), *Rosa Luxemburg Reflections and Writings* (Humanity Books, Amherst, New York: 1999).

For anyone unfamiliar with Marxism, *The Communist Manifesto* by Karl Marx and Frederick Engels is an easy (and short) place to start. There are numerous editions, some with helpful introductions. Donald Sassoon, *One Hundred Years of Socialism: The West European Left in the Twentieth Century* (I B Tauris, London: 1996) is a substantial and always interesting overview of social democracy. Richard Pipes, *Communism A Brief History* (Weidenfeld & Nicholson, London: 2001) is an antagonistic but enlightening canter through the main events and arguments. Richard Gombin, *The Radical Tradition: A Study in Modern Revolutionary Thought* (Methuen, London: 1978) succinctly analyses the divisions between authoritarian and libertarian socialism in theory and practice.

On German socialism, a relatively recent study is Stefan Berger, *Social Democracy and the Working Class in Nineteenth and Twentieth Century Germany* (Longman, London: 2000). Carl E Schorske, *German Social Democracy 1905–1917: the Development of the Great Schism* (Harvard University Press, Cambridge, Mass.: 1983) is worth consulting, covering as it does the period in which Luxemburg was increasingly alienated from the German party. On the crisis in which Luxemburg made her name, see H Tudor and J M Tudor (eds), *Marxism and Social Democracy: The Revisionist Debate 1896–1898* (Cambridge University Press, Cambridge: 1988), a collection of the key contemporary articles and speeches, with a valuable introduction. Manfred B Steger, *The Quest for Evolutionary Socialism: Eduard Bernstein and Social Democracy* (Cambridge University Press, New York: 1997) looks at the chief revisionist. A defence of the theoretician who was at first Luxemburg's mentor and then her enemy is John H Kautsky, *Karl Kautsky: Marxism, Revolution and Democracy* (Transaction Publishers, New Brunswick and London: 1994).

David W Morgan, *The Socialist Left and the German Revolution: A History of the German Independent Social Democratic Party, 1917–1922* (Cornell University Press, Ithaca and London: 1975) remains useful as a study of the party to which Luxemburg's Spartacus League attached after breaking with the SPD. See also Richard J Evans (ed.), *The German Working Class 1888–1933: The Politics of Everyday Life* (Croom Helm, London: 1982), in particular Dick Geary, 'Identifying militancy: The assessment of working-class attitudes towards state and society'.

Luxemburg's relationship with feminism and the women's movement was never straightforward. Raya Dunayevskaya covers interesting ground in *Rosa Luxemburg, Women's Liberation, and Marx's Philosophy of Revolution* (Humanities Press, New Jersey; Harvest Press, Sussex: 1981). Jean H Quataert's *Reluctant feminists in German Social Democracy 1885–1917* (Princeton University Press, Princeton NJ: 1979) and her 'Unequal Partners in an Uneasy Alliance: Women and the Working Class in Imperial Germany', in Marilyn J Boxer and Jean H Quataert (eds), *Socialist Women: European Socialist Feminism in the Nineteenth and Early Twentieth Centuries*, (New York, Elsevier: 1978) fills in the picture. Werner Thönnessen, *The Emancipation of Women: The Rise and Decline of the Women's Movement in German Social Democracy 1863–1933* (Pluto Press, London: 1973) adds further information. Beatrice Farnsworth, *Aleksandra Kollontai: Socialism, Feminism and the Bolshevik Revolution* (Stanford University Press, Stanford, CA: 1980) provides a comparison with a similar figure to Luxemburg, a supporter of the Workers' Opposition in the early years of the Russian Revolution who threw in her lot with Stalin.

Pierre Broué (eds Ian Birchall and Brian Pearce, trans. John Archer), *The German Revolution, 1917–1923* (Brill, Boston, Mass.: 2005) has been rightly praised. There are a number of older but still useful studies including A J Ryder, *The German Revolution of 1918: A Study of German Socialism in War and Revolt* (Cambridge University Press, Cambridge & New York: 1967), F L Carsten, *Revolution in Central Europe 1918–1919* (Temple Smith, London: 1972), and Sebastian Haffner, *Failure of a Revolution: Germany 1918–19* (Andre Deutsch, London: 1973). Chris Harman's *The Lost Revolution, Germany 1918 to 1923* (Bookmarks: London: 1997) is a brisk narrative with a clear political position. Richard M. Watt has a good solid popular history in *The Kings Depart, The Tragedy of Germany: Versailles and the German Revolution* (Phoenix, London: 2003). Alfred Döblin (trans. John E Woods), *Karl & Rosa November 1918 A German Revolution* (Fromm International Publishing Corporation, New York: 1983) is an evocative and highly-regarded fictional interpretation of the revolution and its major characters.

For the broader German historical background, see Geoff Layton, *From Bismarck to Hitler: Germany 1890–1933* (Hodder & Stoughton, London: 2002) and Richard J Evans, *The Coming of the Third Reich* (Penguin/Allen Lane, London: 2003). Useful studies of what followed the revolution and Luxemburg's murder are Eberhard Kolb, *The Weimar Republic* (Routledge, London: 2005) and Ruth Henig, *The Weimar Republic 1919–1933* (Routledge, London: 1998). Ben Fowkes describes the fate of Luxemburg's party in *Communism in Germany under the Weimar Republic* (Macmillan, London: 1984).

Picture Sources

The author and publishers wish to express their thanks to the following sources of illustrative material and/or permission to reproduce it. They will make the proper acknowledgements in future editions in the event that any omissions have occurred.

akg-Images: pp. 74, 98; all other pictures private collections or public domain.

Index